Under His Roof

Malachi O'Doherty

Malachi O'Doherty

15 . 12 . 09 .

SUMMER PALACE PRESS

First published in 2009 by

Summer Palace Press
Cladnageeragh, Kilbeg, Kilcar, County Donegal, Ireland
and
31 Stranmillis Park, Belfast BT9 5AU

LOTTERY FUNDED

Printed by Nicholson & Bass Ltd.

A catalogue record for this book is available
from the British Library

ISBN 978-0-9560995-6-3

This book is printed on elemental chlorine-free paper

for
Ann, Roger, Brian and Niall

Acknowledgments

Some of the material in this book has been published in the *Derry Journal* and the *Belfast Telegraph*. Extracts have been broadcast on Radio Ulster's *Talkback* and *Arts Extra* and read at The Wild Geese Festival, Strangford; The Lonely Page Conference at Queen's University, Belfast; Solstice by the Lough Shore and Aspects Arts Festival, Bangor, County Down.

Biographical Note

Malachi O'Doherty is a journalist and broadcaster based in Belfast. He is the author of four books: *The Trouble with Guns* (Blackstaff 1998); *I Was a Teenage Catholic* (Marino 2003); *The Telling Year* (Gill and Macmillan 2007) and *Empty Pulpits* (Gill and Macmillan 2008).

CONTENTS

'There's going to be changes around here'

Barney would have been fifteen at the time of the Wall Street crash that triggered the great Depression and the Hungry '30s. He left school the year before, insomuch as he had ever been there at all.

So perhaps his fastidiousness, which he failed to pass on to his children, owed as much to an experience of poverty as to the disciplines of the field he later worked in, the bar trade. Even when he had work, it cannot have been very remunerative work.

He said little about those days. A relic of the time was his contempt for farmers. He once surprised me by blurting out a tirade so passionate that there has to have been an untold history behind it. 'When the people starved and had no work, the farmers got their grants. Well, if they are hard up now they can sell their fucking tractors and Range Rovers.'

Maybe he was confusing the '30s with the '80s.

I can't tell if there is any logic to his reading of those periods. He could have been passionate and wrong; indeed, that is what he specialised in.

But he instinctively cared more about those who were doing badly than those who thrived, and not out of some previous induction into socialism either, but out of a sense of justice more like a child's. His disdain for those who mocked the poor was temperamental rather than reasoned, as far as I could see. I often heard others scoff at those who had no jobs but had fridges and television sets. He would have been, at times, too close to the prospect of unemployment himself to want to sneer at those who were overtaken by it. And he knew that he too would have wanted a fridge and a television, if he had little else, and his fags and a noggin of Powers, at the weekend anyway.

The arrivals of fridge and television in our home were both memorable.

The television came first and showed two channels and flickered a lot. In those days, a television set was not expected to work well.

When the fridge came, my mother positioned a kitchen chair in front of it so that she could sit and savour the sight of it. She laughed at herself for doing that. It wasn't much of a fridge. The freezer was just a little box you could make ice cubes in. We never used it for anything else. We imagined we would never be short of ice lollies again.

Possessions then were the fruits of work and saving. And those who were poor, but owned things, were held suspect; they were presumed to be either thriving on welfare benefits by playing the system with skill, or to be crooked in some way or other.

Barney didn't object to people being a little crooked. A man who worked in a bar would often be presented with bargains, things that 'fell off the back of a lorry'. But he knew better than to get roped into returning favours for crooks, so most of the clutter he brought home was promotional stuff that reps had given him, a barometer advertising gin, a cigarette lighter like a Guinness bottle. We had the Black and White dogs on a shelf as an ornament for years, with the name of Buchanan's whisky painted out.

In what sense was Barney poor? He maintained a family of six small children on a barman's pay packet. I was the fourth child, born in Muff, on the Irish border, in County Donegal.

I was the second twin, the third child in a year, and therefore, perhaps, the decider, the one who had made it finally inconceivable that he could stay on in Muff and raise country children. So my mother took us to Ballycastle, where her own parents would be near neighbours and a support.

We got a new terrace house at the foot of an old volcano that the ice age had smoothed the top of. We had a brier ditch between the end of our garden and the wild heather.

My earliest memory of Barney is from then. He is wrestling with a sheep that has fallen into the brier. Even still, when I recall that image, I suffer the remnant of confused emotions: fear for the sheep; the discovery of my father's limitations; fear for him as he huffs and roars, his white hairy leg bleeding through a line of little dots.

Perhaps he had hoped for a time that he would be able to work in Ballycastle. Perhaps Ballycastle had always been just a stepping stone to Belfast. He lived in digs in the city and travelled to visit us on Wednesdays and Sundays. He later moved us all into a house in Belfast, with gardens on three sides of it. And he put six children through school.

Later, when the children got bigger and hungrier, my mother, past having babies, went back to work, at the age of forty-five, as a part-time night staff nurse on a geriatric ward. Now the family could afford a car, and Barney and my mother could have a night together in the pub every week, and we could all have a week's holiday in Donegal, renting a cottage from Barney's sister in Port Salon.

He complained all the time about not having enough money. 'It doesn't grow on trees.' So there would be shouting if he discovered the immersion heater on.

If he had had more money, he could have had nicer clothes and a bigger car. I never once heard him lament the lack of these. When he later had spare money, he just drank more.

To the modern eye, he was poor because he did not own his house. No roof was ever really his. But what people called ownership was only a different payment scheme. The house that he had was small, but no smaller than the houses of his neighbours.

I would not have been able to bear the life that Barney lived when he was my age, serving behind the bar for long days into night, five days a week, and going home to lumps of kids who spent all his money and learned nothing and didn't even understand the burden, let alone share it.

Football

Barney had no interest in football that I saw. Every year, if the sun was out, he would potter about the garden with a radio and listen to the almost shrieked, rapid commentary of Micheál O hEithir on the All Ireland Gaelic football final.

He was not interested in the technicalities of playing style; what use was a radio commentary in conveying that anyway? Barney's investment in a match was his identification with territory. And that has always been a viable investment in Gaelic sports, where players are drawn from local clubs and not bought in. He only had an interest in place.

The first pub in Belfast that he worked in was the Distillery Bar on the Grosvenor Road. This was the bar of the Distillery football team. The distillery itself had closed twenty years earlier, leaving only rare bottles of Dunville malt whiskey and a football team as evidence of its ever having been there.

In the mid 1950s, when Barney was drawing pints for supporters, the team was going through a resurgence. It would be the first club in Belfast to have floodlights. It would win the Ulster cup.

Yet Barney's conversation at the kitchen table was never about the team's achievements. He never took us to any of their matches. His big interests in life, whiskey and roots, were woven together in a sport that most men also get excited about, football. Not him.

The Distillery team had signed Gerry Brennan from Derry in 1952 for £1,000. So there was a connection with home for Barney. Maybe he was just too busy; turning forty, now with five children, living in digs, seeing his family only two days a week. It can't have been a great life. For other men, football was the perfect escape into shared enthusiasm. He appears not to have had that gene.

That Distillery team went on to play Benfica and to draw 3-3 against them. You'd think Barney would have been happy to feel part of such a magnificent local victory.

The last of the old Dunville whiskey now sells at £1,000 a bottle. He would scoff at anyone charging nearly as much for whiskey as for gold, yet later Barney would not have shirked from spending his last tenner on a drink, usually Powers.

Dermot Bolger's novel *A Second Life*, describing a man's struggle with the discovery that he is adopted, includes the secondary theme that football – or attachment to a team – can be the enduring bond between father and son. The bonding magic of football is created by failure as much as by success. The loyal fan is there always, including through the bad times. In Bolger's book, the team is a local one on the local ground – not the big celebrity team of the distant city.

This potential survives in GAA, where the men who take the county into the All Ireland will be known as neighbours and neighbours' children from the streets around the ground they trained in, and where real relationships give fans a more legitimate claim to having been part of the fostering of victory than comes just by virtue of paying for the ticket, wearing the scarf and cheering from the stands.

But perhaps there is a type of man who, even when the conditions are right, as round the distillery in the 1950s, simply doesn't join in, because he does not fit easily into collectives of emotion, whether through shyness or arrogance.

Barney was one of those.

The Fire

We had to fight for heat as children. The fire was the centre of the home, and the whole house, beyond the direct heat from it, was cold.

So you had to push others away to get close, and a demanding sibling could deprive all the others by standing directly in front of the glowing coals. There are myths about the dangers of that to discourage selfishness. You could damage your kidneys or get chilblains.

I remember chilblains as red swelling on the toes or fingers. In our house, it was believed that you got them, not from being cold but from heating up too quickly, after being out in the winter rain without gloves.

We were a big argumentative family, armed with Barney's truculent gene, but what we fought about most was the fire.

Those were chillier times. I remember beds that were like cold water against the skin, sheets that had to be braved, as the edge of the sea is braved by tentative paddlers.

Fire was a constant frustration. I don't know why it was always so difficult to light and maintain. You only have to make sure that the air flows freely through it and that the material itself is flammable and unclogged. We mustn't have been cleaning ours out often enough. I have lit many fires in adult life and I always approach the job with apprehension, recalling the pain of those home fires that didn't burn, yet I've never known a fire since that was as unresponsive to pleading.

Barney tried various devices for starting a sluggish fire. I once saw him trying to light a shoe in the hope it would take the flame and pass it on. He would sprinkle sugar over the coals. When it didn't work he could complain of the poor quality of the coal itself. It is true that it was often damp.

Servicing the fire was servicing the home, and a failed fire was a failure of domestic comfort and order. When he was scooping fat from the pan with a knife and buttering it on to the dusty wet lumps of coal he was illustrating the relationship between bread and fire in a particularly idiosyncratic way.

I learnt later that Hindus ritually serve fire and supply it with cooking oil and food. We had done that for years, not realising the devotional significance. Fire was our god, a fickle god.

The first failure of the flames was expected, like this sullen god's rejection of easy intimacy.

Barney would kneel before the grate and blow at the embers as if he was whispering promises to them. And when that failed he would resort to those dollops of lard or sugar. When offers of obeisance and ritual sacrifice had failed he would take out the larger coals one by one and distribute them around the grate to witness his more humble efforts to light a less ambitious fire.

Fire was impervious to his blandishments and his pleading.

Then he would wall off the whole fireplace with a sheet of newspaper to force the updraught. This sometimes worked. When the fire was weak, you would have to hold the corners of the paper in place, and the problem is that there are four of them and you have only two hands. But then the suction builds and the hot air itself holds the paper.

An interaction starts between fire and this paper wall and the fire preserves the very mechanism that feeds it. This is a marvel for a child to watch. The air roars behind the wall of paper and the flames begin to crackle and show through it. But you mustn't remove the paper too early. Even when it begins to brown in the flames, it may still have more work to do, but you must whisk it away before it takes flame. And that feels like a gloriously dangerous moment, for the fire tugs on the paper.

I have seen Barney bat the paper back into the fire, when he had caught it too late to remove it and it was aflame. Then, just when you thought the whole living room was about to be consumed, the rush of air would carry the burning paper roaring up the chimney.

Yet it should all have been easier than this and less dangerous.

There was a tray under the grate to catch the ash. If the fire had been burning late the night before, this would still be hot to the touch in the morning. If you raked out those ashes you would find red-hot embers among them, so perhaps his preference for leaving them in place stemmed from a sensible aversion to risking the carpet. If fire never obeyed him when he tried to light it, was it not as likely to defy him when he asked it to remain steady on a shovel to be carried out across the room, down the hall and out the front door?

Barney, instead, chanced that the heat in the ash would help the fire from below. It wouldn't. Even hot ashes block the movement of air.

Yet Barney did sometimes seem to have an affinity with fire. He sat guard over it to protect his children – why else would he have crouched so close by it? We never had a fire guard in our house, other than himself.

He could lift by hand little pieces of hot coal that fell onto the tiles. His amazing ability to do this entitled him to the job. I have seen him try to light the fire with a flame carried from the grill in the kitchen on a twist of newspaper, and then smother the last of it by hand when the flame had been passed on to the kindling in the grate.

He might light a cigarette off a similar taper and then, puffing in to take the smoke, he would have no wind to spare on the flame. He would just shake the burning paper in the air around him, creating a carnival of fire and sparks. When I was little he would crouch to tie my shoe lace, blinking with the fag between his lips, no hand free for it, and talk to me through the side of his mouth; 'Hold still there will you, damn you.'

The job had to be rushed so that he could get a finger back to the fag before the static smoke around his face drew a tear or made him cough.

He lived with smoke and fire; he could handle flame. And this gift may have been related in some way to his fiery temper. But fire would not obey him. Fire was frustration. Fire was work. Fire needed constant attention.

Half my father's life's work, it seems, was this waste. The actual product of much of his endeavour was often just a wisp of smoke out of dull damp coal that hardly matched a single sharp intake of breath.

The School Run

I walked a mile to school even when the rain ran off the hem of my duffle coat to redden the bare legs where the soaked wool rubbed them.

But it could be a very bad start to the day if Barney offered his children a lift.

Sometimes he took three of us on the bicycle to school, one on the bar at his knee, another on the carrier behind the saddle and one, most precariously of all, on the handlebars.

I felt no more secure there than a limp unstrapped package would have been because I didn't trust my little bouncing body to stay in place. My fears annoyed him. Why couldn't I simply believe him when he said I would be safe if I didn't move? Because I didn't know how not to move, was too light to have any discernible centre of gravity that could be lowered and secured. It was impossible to be still and he didn't seem to know that.

The most terrifying part of the journey was downhill through Riverdale Park North. The handlebars turned under me on the long corner. Could he not see that I was falling? I could only try to trust that if I did fall he might catch me, or that when he was round the next corner he might free up a hand to shuffle me into a more steady position.

For the plodding second half of the journey, I was dead weight on the bicycle, and he puffed and grunted and cursed the gradient and I had little assurance that he wasn't cursing me too.

Perhaps he gave up doing it that way because he knew we'd eventually crash.

He just stopped cycling altogether when he got a car. He must have sold the bicycle for I don't remember ever seeing it again. But cars created problems too and he had a succession of them that had to be coaxed and tinkered with before they would move at all.

Barney's cars drained as much energy from our little arms and legs as they ever did from fossil fuel.

Some of his older cars had come with starting crank handles in recognition of the need for muscular prompting. You fed one of these in through a hole in the front and turned it in sharp wrenches to get the engine turning.

I could not understand why his later cars didn't have these, they had been so useful. 'Sure don't rush your breakfast; I'll run you to school,' he'd say.

This meant he needed help. The cars were Morris Minors or Ford Anglias or – further back – Austins.

'Sure leave your schoolbags on the back seat.'

Piling them on the footpath would have signalled a hope that he would soon admit failure and let us walk. We might still be on time if we did. While he invested his hopes in his car eventually starting, we invested ours in his admitting an early defeat. Here was a man who wanted to impress his family with his car and a family which didn't even want him to try.

Barney's cars were all horrid, cold and sluggish. They were not designed to be pushed, least of all by small boys. The most likely time for him to need help was on a cold and icy morning. So our bare hands were trying to make an impression on the frosted bodywork while our feet got only a tenuous purchase on the slippery ground. There could be no more thorough way to torture a little boy who wants to imagine himself to be strong enough to meet his father's demands, than to pitch him into vigorous but fruitless work. With the challenge to push-start the car came responsibility for everyone getting to school and for Barney getting to work. And then, when we failed, Barney would berate us for our stupidity and weakness and it would never cross his mind that this was cruelty.

He was dealing with his sons, I imagine, as his own father had dealt with him.

'Christ Almighty!'

He might have been cursing at the car but I always felt included, for what he was really cursing at was the whole circumstance.

There was a slope outside the house, and if you got momentum in the car before you were on that slope, then there was a chance. Barney would run, pushing from behind the door, urging us all on. When the car began to roll, he would leap into the driver's seat to start the ignition. All we needed to do was maintain the speed he had generated. But his own weight, flopping into the seat, would kill the momentum.

'Ach! Can you not get even that right?'

Sometimes we would all get into the car and he would try the ignition again from stationary, just in case our prayers were being heard. I used to imagine that I could will the car to start. Sometimes it worked. I urged from the pit of my stomach as he turned the key. Probably my brothers had similar secret magic. Often it failed.

But occasionally a neighbour, seeing the struggle, would run to help. Two cheery big men might stride in among us when we were preparing another shove. We might grunt a little more volubly to impress them with our eagerness for the task. 'Hold off, Barney, till she's rolling.'

And then these hefty lumps of men would be pushing the car the way it had to be pushed, chuffing and enjoying themselves, smiling encouragement to me as I lent my own negligible weight, so that I could claim a share of the credit just by keeping a hand on the bodywork.

'Grand so, lads. Man dear, that's the way it is done.'

And Barney would be revving the engine to warm it up, while we got into the car to be driven to school – late.

I wonder if the teacher noticed that the only mornings we were late were the mornings we came in the car.

Holidays

Holidays, when we were small, were day trips to Donegal, back to the ancestral homeland for a visit to our relations there.

There were six children in the family then and two parents, so everyone had to take a turn at sitting on someone's knee, or being sat on. This was, fortunately, before the days of mandatory seat belts or restrictions on the amount of alcohol a driver might legitimately have in his bloodstream.

Both my parents enjoyed these trips. My mother planned ahead with lots of buttered rolls for the lay-by breaks, when we'd 'stretch our legs' and the boys would run one way to pee and the girls another.

Barney tended to scowl at the road and at the faces of the children in the rear-view mirror.

'If you can see me in the mirror,' he explained, 'then you are blocking my view.'

But there was never enough room in the car for a head to go elsewhere. And if you squeeze six children onto a seat for two, they will quarrel about their discomfort.

'You can shut up now, or I'll turn round and go back home.'

That would work for a while.

There was no motorway out of Belfast then. The old road through the Sperrins at the Glenshane Pass was narrow and meandering and legendarily dangerous. The city of Derry was so hilly! How could you live in a town where you had to go up a steep hill to go anywhere, or to get back? These were the marvels of travel.

The greatest marvel of all was the Irish border. We would speculate on the danger that the customs man would think we were smugglers. 'Aye, smuggling children. If only I could get a pound for you.'

There is a beach at Buncrana but we children didn't know that and weren't told, or we'd have wanted to go there. The routine was the same every year. Everyone was given some money, and some had savings, so the children were released to walk the main street to buy souvenirs (souvenirs of the day we bought souvenirs – like the Japanese tourist's photograph of a visit to somewhere to have his photograph taken). And mum and dad went to buy gifts for each other and then to the pub.

Toys

Barney often came home with sweets and toys.

We had simple toys then, usually weapons.

The safest of these were the cap pistols. Caps were little spots of gunpowder sealed in paper and they came in strips or in single round tabs. Some of the pistols took a whole strip of dozens of caps, fed up through a mechanism linked to the trigger so that you could repeat-fire dozens of shots without reloading.

Games of cowboys and Indians turned quarrelsome, usually when someone refused to concede that he was dead and lie down.

Bigger boys showed me how you could fire caps in your hand with your thumb and I became adept at this, though I occasionally caused myself spasms of agony when little granules of flaming sulphur got trapped under my nail.

None of this danger suggested to Barney that he shouldn't go on buying us guns for Christmas. Indeed, as we grew bigger and more responsible, at about the age of nine, he would provide us with guns that fired little rods with suction stickers on them and even bows and arrows.

'Don't be pointing at his eyes or I'll take that off you.'

Much safer were the spud guns. You pressed the nozzle into a potato, it extracted a pellet and then the trigger action compressed the air until it popped. These guns were never dangerous enough to hurt but the sharpness of the little explosion was always satisfying.

Older still, we would only be content with guns that could cause actual discomfort, water pistols. The danger in those was that if you fired at somebody bigger than you, he would come and hit you. And if you fired at your brothers and soaked their clothes, your mother or Barney would take it away.

Later, when Barney started allocating pocket money, with the admonition that we now had to acquire responsibility and learn to save, the moral tuition turned out to be a waste of breath.

'Daddy, can I have mine now?'

'It's not due until Friday.'

'But the new *Dandy* is out.'

And with a grunt, he would reach into his pocket and present a shilling on the flat of his palm. Part of the game was to say nothing, to act as if he was only showing it to you, but you grabbed it and hugged him.

And then you got your full pocket money on a Friday anyway, the loan forgotten.

Warm times came often with the fragrance of alcohol on the breath. Even after all the worst of it since, the smell of drink brings the promise of love and generosity. And a little excitement, possibly dangerous.

Wednesday nights were, for a time, nights of special joy, when he took my mother to the pub and they came noisily home and woke us all up and showered the beds with packets of potato crisps.

Mostly we were expected to find our own fun though. We were turned out onto the streets and building sites and fields to run wild until teatime. And recalling that, I can't think I would chance it with any child today, or could have been happy myself without it.

Donegal

What we liked about Donegal was that it was primitive, scruffy and lawless. That seemed to explain Barney; that he had come out of a culture and was not uniquely anarchic.

When we crossed the border into Donegal on our holidays, we always felt ourselves relaxing, spontaneously; the checkpoint behind us, freedom ahead.

There are some who report that sensation as evidence of the North having been a fearful police state, so horrid to live in that the very air was oppressive. But I am talking about a time before the Troubles, when the border was an easy crossing. Still, we would have built it up in our minds into a challenge, like Checkpoint Charlie, where a grim and gruesome official with a gun might decide to disrupt the holiday, but usually a lazy customs officer just waved us through without looking at us.

'Shush now,' Barney would say, if the B Specials were checking cars leaving the jurisdiction. They just looked like policemen to me, and though I remember us all tensing with apprehension I do not remember them being rude.

The sense of relief on entering Donegal was about the imagined first smell of a distant sea; it was also about a general air of dilapidation which told you that the values of tidiness that constrain a child did not apply there.

We came to associate the smell of turf with that feeling of giddy release, and I always cheer up still when I catch a whiff of it.

This county was different in other ways, and we romanticised them. Running water and electricity were not dependable.

From the mid-60s, we would go every year to Aunt Ena's cottage in Port Salon, where an influx of eight people would so overstrain the plumbing that we would, after the first day, all have to go to the toilet in the hedges and ditches, or hold tight until we got to the hotel.

The hotel itself was a relaxed space. There was no rule against children being in the bar. Closing times were theoretical.

It was here in Donegal that Barney, as a child, had come to understand that laws are not binding on people who are enjoying themselves.

Even in the 1980s it was common to see battered old cars without number-plates on the roads of Donegal. I knew a teacher in south Donegal who used to drive into town along the white line, so that he could keep himself from bouncing off the kerbs while drunk.

When I lived there for a time myself, I signed on the dole, and if I missed a week because I was off hitchhiking, the clerk would forge my signature and keep the money for me.

All of this resonated with my understanding of Barney, who thought you obsessive and absurd if you took a rule literally.

There were grim solitary old men around Donegal. A man in the country dressed differently. These men wore black suits all the time and rode big black bicycles. Some of them were astonishingly strong from walking over hills after scattered sheep and digging their own turf.

Some of them were broken by poverty and loneliness. You would see one of them drink himself senseless in the hotel and the barman ask around for someone to get him home. Barney might have turned into one of these had he not, against the odds, found his way into a marriage and a family in his 30s, after the war.

Looked at that way, the children that he scowled at, the wife whose spirit he broke, were the saving of him.

We often went back to Donegal to be assured that it was still the playground it had been for Barney as a child.

But I also learnt there, that you were no one unless you owned a little bit of the ground. And we didn't. There was still a time, thirty years ago, when you could buy an old cottage for a few hundred pounds. Looking back, it seems mere insanity not to have done so. Everyone else did – nearly everyone else. We went to Donegal to abandon all sense of being bound by practical necessity. That was not how others went there; it was not how most people there lived.

I remember sitting in an aunt's house counting the holy pictures and statues and getting up to sixteen in the one room. People were ostentatiously religious and spoke all the time of God's will and of being 'spared'. But in the garage or shed there would be an oily man with cuts on his hands and arms, who worked relentlessly on engines or stone walls to lay the basis of a future fortune. He wasn't waiting for God to fashion his life. Nor was he bound by many of the Ten Commandments.

It is a hard place and it was little wonder that when you commented to a local on the beauty of the sunset, he thought you a bit touched, for you can't buy or sell the evening light – though you can work for longer by it without using up electricity.

Barney would not have thrived well there. He wasn't the oldest son. He didn't have land. He worked as a barman. He could have survived if he had had his own pub. That was his vocation.

But he would have been too old to enjoy the transformation of Donegal in the 1990s, when property wealth cleaned it up and made it more orderly. I told him once that I'd been to Pat McKenna's shop in Muff, next door to the house I was born in. There were now gaming machines beside the rows of groceries, a natural extension of selling lottery tickets. 'Who uses them?' he said, perplexed.

He had known bars where the only food was a white bread sandwich with a slab of processed cheese and a dollop of pickle from a jar. Now, old stone buildings that someone had forgotten to knock down are restaurants serving oysters with Guinness. His generation would have been sceptical about oysters and alarmed at the thought of eating mussels. How could they be clean?

Shopping

The Donegal shop of my father's youth was of a type that survived into my own, before almost disappearing.

There was one in Dore in northwest Donegal, where I went on the Gaeltacht in 1963. It was a big brick shed with a long wooden counter. A child's interest was in Cidona and Tiffany, the drinks and chocolate bars that we never saw at home. Behind the counter was an array of boxes for nails and chemicals. I knew Alum from my chemistry set but did not understand why anyone would want the stuff.

A shop like this had to anticipate every need that might arise this side of the mountain range, whether for a plaster for a cut or plaster for the wall; for a shovel or a piece of satin ribbon. Some shops doubled up as pubs. One like this was Rita's in Port Salon. Barney was more attracted by Rita's and its echo of old Donegal than by the sea, which he never dipped a foot in; or the sand, which he never walked on. He looked down on the beach with patriarchal satisfaction that it was still there, and that was the height of his interest in it.

Rita sold cigarettes, pots and pans, washing-up liquid and standard groceries over the half of the counter near the door. Down the other end, she sold drink. Irish licensing laws, or the lack of them, allowed this spread. And local culture saw nothing wrong with children coming in to buy sweets beside a tired farmer having a pint.

In the suburbs, as in towns, shops could specialise and even compete with each other over who got to sell newspapers and cigarettes. But when we moved on to the housing estate on the edge of Belfast in the 1950s, we were serviced first by vans. Stewart's van came round on a Friday evening, a mobile shop that compressed variety. It must have taken some kind of genius to anticipate what we would want and how much, but perhaps we were all too poor and too similar for that to be a challenge.

And, of course, our mothers didn't want a choice of a dozen different washing powders, some biological, some not. They wanted Tide, Persil, Omo or Daz, and they were not fussed about a blue whitener for they knew how to add it themselves in the bucket.

Throughout the week, the streets were serviced by a range of traders. A man in a turban came on a bicycle to sell plastic brushes. The rag man came with his horse and cart to gather in old clothes and give out balloons for them. And another man sold sticks for the fire.

The rent man and the insurance man called at the house too.

We were like settlers of the West on that new estate, pioneers who had plonked ourselves at the heart of a sprawling building site, so far from the centre that we had to walk a mile to the bus terminus.

The first big shop that I was aware of was Woolworths. Barney would take us downtown to explore it, as a father might now take his children to a science park. There you got to pick and mix sweets of your choice and handle cap pistols and spud guns and even spring-loaded hand grenades. Conscientious about school, we lusted over plastic rulers and pencil sets, some that were too flash to be seen on your desk.

Later, shopping had become a form of entertainment for everyone, not just for children. The first step in this evolution was towards window-shopping, where the objective was simply to look at what was on display, to imagine yourself owning it. Then along came credit.

An early form was administered through the Catalogue. One of the neighbours would have jurisdiction over the floppy big book of coloured pictures of everything you could possibly want, from a child's tricycle to a bra. You would order from her and pay the instalments week by week. And there was hire purchase, by which you rented your goods long enough to have paid for them. These were ways in which merchandisers could shift the risk of not being paid, while you could have today what you could afford tomorrow.

I visited Barney one day and asked him how he was getting on with the garden. He moaned that he was getting too old for it. I lifted his spade and was amazed by how heavy it was. I took him to buy a new, lighter model, confident that the technology for making these things would have improved in the last fifty years. Barney had not known that the big shop that sold everything had come back.

We went to a prefabricated building the size of an aircraft hangar that could have sold us a floor or a chandelier.

Pets

He hated cats.

They spread TB. He wouldn't have a dog in the house either, but he wouldn't even have had a cat in the coal shed.

Barney was a Donegal peasant who had refined his manners enough for the city back streets and the pub and no further. He was from among people who were plain and harsh.

If he had wanted a cat for catching mice he'd have gone to a neighbour.

'Have you drowned that litter yet?' he'd have said. 'Well, leave one out of the bag for me, will you.'

He tolerated dogs but he laughed at advertisements for dog food. When he had a big family at home with its inevitable leftovers, why would he buy canned meat for a dog, to prolong its active life or for any other purpose?

We had a succession of dogs. The first I remember was a big black hairy mongrel called Tito, after Marshal Tito of Yugoslavia.

Tito was with us in Ballycastle when we were small enough to sit astride him. I have a recollection of wondering why his back sank under me and he wouldn't try to hold me – probably because he had more sense than I had.

In Belfast we had gardens on three sides of the house and plenty of room for dogs to play in. The first, I think, was a little black and tan pup, probably at least part Alsatian. It whimpered and wailed in the coal shed for hours.

Barney liked having dogs about him, but he had nothing like actual love for them. The shed in which they were kept was a tiny outhouse, one half of which stored the coal and the other half of which was shelved for tools and the sort of junk that wouldn't get thrown out altogether. It was in the porch by the front door and there was no window or light of any kind. The floor was cement and the walls were plain brick. The whole inside was blackened by years of coal dust, but this was made into a home for the dog, with an old hessian sack for it to sleep on. As a sensitive child, I fretted almost as much as the pup did, but it was explained to me that they don't feel things the way we do – they only sound like they do.

The wailings of some beasts do not touch human hearts; the wailings of dogs do.

Where other children hugged and kissed their pets, and even kept them in their homes and let them sleep on their beds, we had a more realistic sense that animals were dirty and insensitive brutes that could be amusing but had to be kept separate from us.

Barney fed these dogs on plate scrapings, potato peelings, stale bread and cold tea, and they lapped it as enthusiastically as any other dog in the street might gorge on Pedigree Chum.

The dog's plate was often an old bar tray, never a bowl.

The first time I saw an animal fed leftovers from a dinner plate was in England and the logic that the plate would be washed, and that therefore no essential rule of hygiene had been broken, simply failed to override the understanding imbued in me by my father about the need for distance between humans and animals.

Our dogs never complained. Indeed they were happy running wild about the garden with us and they would bound cheerfully into the coal shed when the door was opened for them at night.

Yet none of them lived long. We always knew a dog's time was up when it started to cough. These were dry hacking coughs that disturbed the creature's whole body.

And the bounce would go out of the beast as the grip of distemper tightened.

Barney would not even consider calling a vet but he had sufficient concern to try his own remedies.

Once he poured whiskey – or a liquid like it from a little Powers bottle – down the throat of Rusty, one of the dogs I remember best, and Rusty leapt several feet into the air, howling at the shock. He hadn't even drawn breath to shriek but produced the noise from the eruption of fundamental panic in his gut. Perhaps this was a remedy Barney had heard from a man in the bar. It did nothing for the dog.

We never had a dog die of old age or get run over, though one, a lovely tan pup called Shane, disappeared and we speculated that he had been stolen for medical experiments.

Another, I took for some reason to the USPCA to be put down. I sat at the front of the bus with the dog in a box and proudly told everyone I met about my serious mission. I had no sense that this was anything but the normal way to dispose of a dog you didn't want any more.

Barney's attitude to dogs changed a little in his old age. He acquired a pedigree Alsatian, a big scary looking dog with dippy haunches that would have taken fright at a spider. This was a dog with a long name and a number. When it blocked the path, I was afraid to go past it at first, until I realised that it could not have been more docile if it was drunk.

This dog lived in an improvised kennel, a structure like those we as children would have erected as a playhouse, a leaky low lean-to in the back garden. And Long-Number had pups.

One rainy day, I was sitting with Barney, talking about politics or scowling at the television.

'Will you have a coffee? Well, put the kettle on; you know where it is. Your arm's not broke.'

Suddenly the dog was scraping frantically at the back door, which opened directly onto the garden. Barney opened the door to pacify the dog but, against all past discipline, she rushed past him into the living room with one of the wee blind, whimpering pups in her mouth.

Oblivious to Barney's fulminating, the dog brought six pups into the house, out of the wet cold shack that was home, and deposited them on the warm sofa. 'Did you ever see the like of that?' he said. 'That dog's mad.'

This was the extent to which he would marvel at the tenacity of the maternal instinct in a dumb animal.

He would shout at his dogs and push them away, swipe at them with a stick, and they would reward him with panting enthusiasm for his attention and a long wet tongue. And this was no mystery to Barney at all.

Fathering

In Barney's day, a father did not have much responsibility for children. He was a background presence, a shadow.

In cowboy films, Pa would ask the boy what 'chores' he would do for the day. The boy would ride out to Ma Connolly's place and see if she needed a fence fixed and then he would come home with one of her apple pies. Life was wholesome and busy in a fictional realm; in our own, children squandered days in play and fathers strode past to work or joined in occasionally, as a rare treat – to kick a ball or show how to paste pictures into a scrapbook – and then went back to more important things, adult things.

Barney wouldn't have gone along with the idea that you should talk to your children as if they are thoughtful and intelligent people, give them all the ideas they can absorb, answer all their questions.

He enjoyed the fresh naivety of children, and he toyed with it when he could. He was nostalgic for our innocence and pliability when we grew up. We had been an audience for his instinctive playfulness. His late unhappiness may have come out of his need to suppress his dramatic tendencies, his failure to find expression for clowning.

So, when we were small, we believed in Santa Claus and God. There was an understanding in Barney, not shared with us until much later, that we would eventually let go of both, though not at the same time. A father like Barney expected his children to lose Santa at about ten years old and never to stop believing in God, but to have the good sense to stop bending to His will, as interpreted by churchmen, before the age of twenty.

Growing up, therefore, was a progression from a fantasy world into a concrete world in which consequences were taken seriously and in which one serious consequence of retaining fantasies that should have expired, was that other men thought you a fool.

I doubt if Barney could have quoted Ecclesiastes or Saint Paul, but he understood fundamentally that beliefs have their season and that 'childish things' were to be put away to enable a man to think as a man.

Another more literate parent would have attended to what a child was reading, so that books might always be right for the little one's level of maturity. Barney left that to my mother. But when he once remarked on a book looking as if it was 'too old' for me, she cut across him and told him, effectively, that he didn't know what he was talking about.

Children, in his view, should not speak like adults. I never heard Barney swear until I was working with him in the bars, and it appalled me. He reprimanded us as children if we brought playground language into the home.

A boy has to learn the gradations of offence in the rough words, and he may get these wrong at first. 'Shit' is a stronger word than 'Shite', for instance.

More coyly, as small children, we'd call the bum 'the bottom' and the bottom the 'b-t-m'. When I first, at school, heard it called 'the hole', I thought that a good imaginative usage, an innocent word, creatively deployed. When I repeated it at the kitchen table, Barney exploded in a way in which he would not have done had I said, 'your bum!'

'I don't know what that school's teaching you.'

We had our childish words for the respective male and female organs of urination. When we had no idea they had any other function, they were the 'tail' and the 'toot'. Still, we knew that discussing the puzzle of why they should be different could get you sharply reprimanded. Indeed, we wouldn't have known there was anything smutty about the subject in the first place, apart from the toiletry implications, if not for the anger these queries provoked.

Language hardened as we grew older. There would be a time when the word 'fuck' would be allowed in conversation with Barney outside the house, and then later it would be unselfconsciously deployed by everyone, inside and out.

The other graded activities were drinking and smoking. I first tasted whiskey on my mother's knee. I had come downstairs with a toothache and Barney had suggested a wee drop. It burned my tongue. At sixteen, we were allowed a glass of beer on holidays in Donegal. But when, one night, at about seventeen, I came home from work in a bar and threw up six bottles of Piper and a packet of KP nuts over the bathroom floor, Barney was livid. He hadn't sufficient empathy with my own shame and horror – and wooziness – to let me sleep, but bellowed at me that I had no right to come 'gargled' back to his house, and I had better learn to accept that.

Smoking was easier to negotiate. It only gave you cancer; it didn't make you sick. And while every one of us hid our early smoking from him, every time the secret came out, it was accepted as an established fact. Since you were now presumed to be an addict too, there was no point in lecturing you.

Once, after I had given up smoking for two weeks, on one stressful night of the Troubles, Barney handed me a fag to soothe my nerves and put me back on them.

We had grown up with smoke all around us. Nothing was more inevitable than that, at the right time, we would start to inhale. Maturity, to us, was taking things at their due time, and not before. It was the boys and girls who smoked and drank and groped behind the shops at fourteen or fifteen, who were the rough ones, the bad types. We were different, not in that we shunned those things, only in that we deferred them, in order to be children a little longer – the way Barney liked us.

Smoking

Barney knew with the same clarity that he knew most things that smoking is bad for you. He didn't need to hear it on the *Nine O'Clock News*. His own sisters, attacking his early aspiration to be a man, told him the fags would 'stunt his growth'.

Long before anyone had connected smoking to cancer, people had known that it was expensive, addictive and made you cough – all good reasons in themselves for inhaling nothing but air.

Barney's generation took to smoking, not out of ignorance of the damage fags would do, but in spite of the threat of corrosion and depletion. That generation accepted the trade-off – or most of it did.

Of course, they made the judgement early, when they were children, and when the rewards were of a type a child would value. Later, when it made more sense not to smoke, the challenge to stop would reveal itself as insurmountable.

Barney probably started smoking in 1928. I don't know who he was modelling himself on. Later, a thousand surly men in black and white movies would express their varied attitudes by the way they handled a cigarette or stubbed the life out of the last glow in the ash. Smoking was a gift to early cinema directors. Puffing, blowing or talking through the smoke with a fag in the teeth, widened the range of expressions a face could muster.

Impressionable young people were turned in the direction of an early grave by Bogart or Bacall, but Bogart would have been late for Barney. His first film wasn't until 1936.

So perhaps the model was his own father, or a farm boy, or the sailors coming off the boats on Derry docks, or just his own peers at school. People then endorsed the efforts of boys to look like men and took them out of childhood early. The young apprentice showed his willingness to learn by dressing like his master and walking like his master so why not also by smoking like his master?

Smoking was a normal manly comfort like long trousers, but a boy who started early could be teased about racing ahead of his years. He would be assured though that there would come a time at which he was fully grown and could safely smoke all he liked.

But why was it all right for men to struggle with addiction? No one who smoked surely failed to register the need it wrote into the nerves of the throat.

When I started smoking as a teenager, Barney was indulgent. He took the view that I was old enough to know better and that if I, despite that, had lashed my life to a compulsion that would both poison and impoverish me, then that was my business.

He would have been more uncomfortable with teenage sons who had succeeded in rejecting his lifestyle completely. Now we could share a fag together, like men – confident that my mother, who smoked too, would disapprove.

She hated the presumption that she was in no place to criticise, being addicted herself. She was well placed to say what was wrong with smoking, since it was choking her. By the time she was forty she had been prescribed a thin stick bristle brush for her gullet. It appalled and amazed me that she could get it down her throat. She said that her doctor had advised her to change her brand to Kensitas. She had a leg amputated in her mid-60s after smoking-related circulation problems had produced gangrene, and she died of emphysema when she was seventy. Barney would out-smoke her by seventeen years.

Barney had grown up in a cloud of grey smoke. I grew up in that same cloud. I did not notice it because it was normal to me. I would not have been able to tell you at fifteen that that was the smell of smoke – it was just the smell of people. The teachers in school had smelt of the same mustiness. It was those who were fresh and fragrant who were strange.

Most men had brown stains between their fingers and on their thumbs. Smoking seemed to connect a man to the earth. Wrestling with toxic smoke in the throat and lungs connected a man to his body in much the same way as wrestling with weights does. It reminds him with less effort that he is physical. You could see it in the way Barney sat, bunched into himself; in the way he stood, slouched onto his hip, like someone who favoured discomfort. You saw it in the way he drank, and rubbed his lips with the back of his hand. There was a hint of it too in his favourite drink being neat whiskey. This was a man for whom gripping tangible heat in his throat was confirmation that he existed.

Teenagers in the House

Barney's derision might emerge as amusement or a scowl. The smile was more effective for its rarity. Faced with it, I would warm to him immediately, like someone who, with the sun out, can now take off a drab coat.

I have often wondered what the turning point was from his softer fathering to his dogmatic patriarchal manner. In a sense, he had been a new man before other new men. He had been soft and gentle and funny with his little boys.

In their mid-thirties my mother and father had no children. In their mid-forties they had six. Barney was a rudimentary father. He did the basics. He housed, fed and clothed those children and, when they were young, he was glad to do that. He thought it was enough to be proud of. For a child, the present is the eternal condition of things. Children don't notice that what is enduring by their view may be seen by their parents as a sudden change in their circumstances and that they may still be reeling from the shock.

In Barney's mid-fifties the children were all loud demanding teenagers. He didn't understand them nor they him. It never occurred to me that he had done something heroic and that I ought to be grateful, though I have known all my life that I could not have done as much myself.

I have felt a guilty sense that we turned on him, stopped playing Horsey on his knees, stopped kissing him, stopped calling him Daddy. I feel also that he turned on us. And there may have been other spoilers of that love.

For one thing, he was a born alcoholic. It may be that when he had small children and no money he was a better man because he was drinking less.

He used to bring home, every Friday night, a little iron model animal and we built a zoo on the mantelpiece, before there was a television. Maybe the turning point was the Troubles, for they angered and worried him, as they would have angered and worried any father of teenage sons in a city that consumed itself. But I believe the real trouble for him was his boys passing into adolescence. That transition would have been hard for him in peacetime too.

Maybe the change was in his simply being with us more often.

As a barman in Belfast, while we lived in Ballycastle, every visit home to us must have felt like a relief and a holiday. In those days, he didn't own a car, so the bus journey home was long and broken, through narrow country roads.

But once he was living with us full-time, we were no longer novel, but often boring, irritating and loud.

He had had these children and bathed them and changed their nappies. Then one day, without warning, he would walk into the bathroom, and one of them would shriek at him to get out. It was not he who had changed the rule.

He had stories from our early childhood that he repeated as evidence that he had once loved us and that we had needed him.

Once, he said, he could find no match in the house in Muff to light the gas to heat our bottles so he unscrewed the base of the electric iron and took a light on a scrap of torn paper from the reddening element inside.

'Aye, to light your fag by, more like,' says the cynical mind. In his version there was no fag, but of course there was.

When my mother was in hospital and we were small children, he did the cooking, and not very well. But I recall the taste of fried spam with wonder still.

Men of my generation learned painfully to be unlike our fathers. We were taught by the feminists to discard the old gruffness and assumption of seniority. But Barney's development had gone, I think, in the other direction.

Or maybe I have remembered all this wrongly. Maybe the exciting and memorable pleasures impressed because they were rare. A father who worked long hours, and who worked, when we were small, in another town, acquired the air of legend. He existed more in anticipation than as a physical presence.

And it wasn't always a good fresh anticipation. A remote father doubled up as a bogeyman or Bad Wolf. 'Wait till your father gets home.'

Manhood

I was not a man by my father's understanding of what a man is – nor was I going to be one.

This does not mean that he did not sometimes appear to love and even admire me. His conception of manhood and its contrast with what I was, could be a discomfort to him as much as to me. And like all people, he moved between periods of confidence and insecurity – and one of the ideas that rose up to torture him when he was insecure, was that a real man is a strong, resolute and dependable creature – such as he would insist on being himself, such as he would expect his sons to be. Except that we weren't.

It's pointless to ask where his notions of manhood came from. They were once almost universal.

For Barney, silence was strength. Yet he was often bullish and assertive. He swaggered and bragged. When he couldn't assert himself, he would fall back into a more narrow self which scowled at the world. The phrase I remember hearing him use most often is, 'there's going to be changes round here.' And of course, he was the man who would make them. Another was, 'you were less trouble when you were small.' He was nostalgic for a time when he had had little children who rode on his knees and gave him goodnight kisses on the lips, who trotted beside him to keep level with his walking pace and thought him only marvellous. 'God knows what's become of you.'

His model of manhood from cinema was John Wayne. He loved that decisive sock-on-the-jaw moment in those films. Clark Gable's way to sweep a woman off her feet was to kick her heels out from under her. John Wayne's too. Barney loved *The Quiet Man* with its interminable and implausible fight scene. Any man who punched another man's face that much would kill him and smash his own knuckles. In the film, the contenders could stop for a drink and then resume. It was all nonsense. But it was a celebration of male bonding around assertive violence, drink and the power to control women. There was no question but that this was the completion of the masculine urge. And warmth from a real man, expressed minimally, was amplified by a sense of power restrained. This was how Barney saw himself in an ideal world, and his suffering and anxiety derived from his failure to measure up to it.

And if the failure of his sons to turn into strong hard men was no corrective to this ideal, then ageing should have been. Yet he tried to start a fight in a bar in his eighties when even he must have acknowledged that the years had weakened him.

I had been trying to befriend him by taking him for a drink every Sunday night.

Once, he judged that a man at another table was staring at him so he started staring back. There was a further exchange of stares when we got up to leave, and suddenly Barney was arched forward, his coat open, rubbing his hands and ready to take on this challenger; and in a stupid way, like he was spreading himself to let the other guy have the first blow, the way you would masquerade with a child. That was probably the only kind of fighting he really knew.

It's the only type I know.

I had to drag him from the bar. And that left him with the consoling fantasy that he could have taught that man a lesson if he'd been allowed to; he had not backed away.

And in that truculent state, he would be difficult to take home.

I called a taxi and told the driver that my father was drunk and argumentative and that if he would accept all his abuse and say nothing I would give him a good tip. We stuck to that arrangement for weeks.

But I inherited my father's vanity.

Once, I told him about a scare I had had in Paris. I had been coming up the escalator from the Metro when a group of young men surrounded me and started going through my pockets. They were sneak thieves who would have understood that they had already botched their job when they let me feel their hands about me. I spun round shouting and swinging my bags at them. They withdrew laughing.

In the version I gave Barney, I had kicked and scattered them. 'So? It's what I'd expect,' he said. 'It's nothing. You are an O'Doherty.'

You got derision if you weren't a fighter but only minimal acknowledgement that things were as they should be, if you were. I was blood of his blood and in some ludicrous family legend, a fighting man too.

Barney had a swagger that I copied once on the street, when I was accosted by one of the drunks who hang around Castle Court scrounging pennies. The man had himself affected to be trying to steal my bicycle but, in fact, hardly knew where he was. I didn't want to push him or start a clumsy wrestling match so I did what I had seen Barney do. I stepped back to size him up. I duked to the right and to the left. I studied the palms of my hands, spat in one, clasped and rubbed them together, shook myself down as if checking that my trousers were still up, all the time eyeing him fast. Before the act was finished, the man had backed away and, to my amazement, a frantic woman was screaming at me to leave him alone.

I would never have chanced that performance with a man who had looked like he really was up for a fight.

Barney even directed his rage at inanimate things. One night we were awakened by a clatter from below. When I got downstairs I saw him in a state of shock where a wax fly strip, which was so heavy he should not have taped it to the ceiling, had fallen onto the Belleek tea set, a wedding present for him and my mother.

He was arched in vest and underpants flinging the damned fly strip into the fireplace and cursing at it.

But the damage was his fault.

Our lives had been darkened by the fear of knocking over that tea set as we had played around it since we were toddlers. Maybe Barney felt that a sufficiently fierce and direct attack on the fly strip would deflect attention away from his carelessness.

And I was embarrassed for him for I knew how much trouble we would be in ourselves for being stupid enough to tape the fly strip of Damocles in place.

Barney would be left with only his own conscience to accuse him, and I understood that that would be worse than taking a berating.

He was afflicted by an inherited requirement that he be master in his own house and with a sense of fundamental failure as a man if he wasn't: this in an age which left him no resources with which to enforce his rule.

The long war between us grew into an uneasy truce. He could not make us need him. The more he tried, the more he pushed us away.

I felt he expected me to say something that might end the war between us but I had no idea what that should be. For want of my saying it, he would judge that I had misunderstood him.

He often eyed me with the confidence that he knew me better than I knew myself, as if he was just waiting for me to stop pretending that I wasn't still his child.

Those who treat alcoholism say that the drinker stops growing wiser at the point at which drink comes to be used to numb the sort of pain that should make you think again. Barney started drinking at about twelve or thirteen, I guess, for part of him was never more mature than that. And he got by in life because everyone loves a little boy.

When he lay in hospital, close to the end, a man called Marty came to visit. He sat beside me at the end of the bed. He said, 'See that man there? That man is a gem.'

Barney had had charms that would light up the lives of other men. And when he opened his eyes and saw Marty there, he came alive with interest in a way that he never did with me.

Education

Barney was uncomfortable about how education distanced his sons from him. He should not have been. We were not highly educated but we thought we were and, worse, he thought we were.

When we went to metalwork class the teacher taught us to make serviette rings. We'd bring them home to a mother who would admire them and a father who would wonder why we weren't making something useful. We'd never had serviettes in our house.

He had left school at fourteen and had not been there much anyway. So he didn't read books and he couldn't help much with homework except in one area, sums. He was brilliant at what was then called mental arithmetic. It was still called that in a chapter of the textbook we used at school, but we worked out our sums on paper, not in our heads. He had been totting up bar bills in his head for decades and was fast. He could look over my shoulder as I laboured with my homework and spot my mistakes instantly.

He was a dark shadow over me.

But if I asked him for help he could give little. He would know what the answer to a question was but he could not describe the process by which he had reached it. And it was perhaps this impatience with himself as much as with us that generated the anger. But anger it was.

His concern that we would turn out more clever than he was prompted him to cheer at all evidence that we wouldn't. He scoffed at our stupidity when he saw it. 'God, you're not so smart at all when it comes down to it.' I think these little evidences of inadequacy in us reassured him that he was better than us, and in his more generous moods, that he could be of value to us.

What riled him was the language we used in arguments and discussions. It may be that he was much further behind us in reading and writing than he let on. He never, that I saw, read a book. He never in his life wrote me a letter. I don't know for sure that he could read and write well at all. Nor, however, did he ever look up from his paper and ask what some obscure word meant.

The unease about having literate sons exacerbated, I suspect, a division in his marriage. Mum was a trained nurse and could help us with homework, not just with English and sums but with Latin and Geography too. Teachers expected us to get nightly homework signed by a parent and when she was out at work he would do that. I believe his reaction was complex. Ask him to sign it and he would demur. But I think he often held the homework book in his hand with pride in us. His fear of being outstripped wasn't a consistent background annoyance. It just flared up when he was insecure.

In bed at night, when we could hear them arguing in the next room, we could often make out jibes about us being spoiled and useless. We weren't men at all.

By his own values, he was right.

We were sweet-faced swots, late to puberty and late to shaving, stunted by bookishness, unlike the rough lads who were more familiar to Barney, snarly boys who smoked and said 'fuck' a lot. School had divided young people and created a type that was soft and wordy, that didn't fight. At eighteen, I could not drive a car let alone strip an engine. I could do nothing of any particular practical value. Well, I could turn up the legs of my trousers, for my mother had taught me to sew. Subversively?

Barney could look around at young men who had left school and taken jobs, and he could see that they were more rugged and decisive, that they owned cars and tinkered with them. They would go to the pub with their fathers on a Friday night and, informed by the same fatigue, enjoy their beer with the same thirst. It was all very well feeding ungrateful and useless sons if they were going to be teachers or doctors. But what chance was there of that? We didn't even believe that ourselves.

Many men must have felt embarrassed by sons being educated beyond where they could follow. We were in the first generation to have free education. Without it, we would have been bringing money into the house at fifteen, as he had. No previous man in Barney's family had ever had to go on supporting boys who were fit to work and would plainly benefit from working, and be stronger and more like other men if they did. This was an inevitable annoyance. But how grateful were we? Not at all. We argued with him constantly.

My generation had it easy in one respect; our parents couldn't see what intellectual frauds we were. When I later met people who had high achieving and educated parents, I found that they were burdened by expectations that had never bothered me.

Temper

Barney should have understood the Buddhist maxim that anger is a 'losing throw'. He had had enough experience. No one who easily succumbs to spontaneous rage would fail to have learnt that much. A short temper may feel like an exultant sprint to a winning line, but it rarely gets there. The angry man enjoys overwhelming satisfaction in being right but confidence overtakes him and makes a fool of him. And no matter how often this confidence is exposed as the trickster who leads him to humiliation, he never loses faith in it.

His contentment with being right only turns to anger when it is well challenged.

Anger is panic. I know this so well because I have inherited it from Barney. I have that same delight in imagining a day on which I will have the last word and settle everything on my terms.

I am thrilled by verbosity, by cutting eloquence. I was never to be the man who would settle scores with violence or a fist slammed on a table. Therefore my weapon would be the word that is so apt that I cannot help but admire my own use of it.

I think Barney usually feared he was wrong and therefore lighted too enthusiastically on the occasional, apparent breaks in that pattern. You would see it in his eye – that chuffed look, as if he had just discovered a cure for piles and was about to restore the equanimity of half the human race. And no matter how often he was proved wrong, he never gave up his faith in an innate right to be right. The alternative was to admit that he was always wrong, and about everything.

He should have shored up his morale by counting the things he was sure about, that were beyond challenge. These were the little things.

His conversation always started tentatively.

'No heat,' he would say. He would not expect to get an argument out of the weather.

'You're right there, Barney,' the passerby would say. But if the passerby would stop, Barney would move on to more specific statements, to see if agreement on these was as easy, such as that some politician was a chump.

'Jamie to Christ, did you ever hear the likes of it?' He'd be inviting and enjoying argument on a matter that was neutral between them, an object or issue they could share contempt for.

Conversations like these were the fodder of his assuredness that he was a man who understood the world. He was enjoying concurrence with others on the common lore, about the weather and politics. But the common lore is simplistic and often wrong.

'The only way this trouble will end now is with a United Ireland,' he would say. Well, the men in the pub had agreed on that.

'Can't see how it would come about,' I'd say. 'Does Dublin really want it?'

Challenged to reconsider, at the very moment of his highest confidence, Barney would thump the table. 'Hell damn Dublin! Has Dublin got the last word?'

And it would be better to concede perhaps that it hadn't, but instead, a boy with his genes and his needs will have scented his own prospect of being right, and battle would commence, for dignity and self respect.

He shocked me when I came home in my late twenties after years away. I had forgotten how demanding he was. We were having a little drink to welcome me home. Actually, he'd have been having a little drink even if I was still away. He was explaining drug addiction to me. He said, the more you took the more you needed; what got you high at first, no longer worked. I can't imagine how he could have known about this, for there was no significant drug culture around us then, apart from alcoholism. But I had smoked cannabis so I explained that it was the exception to the rule. Once you were familiar with its intriguing vapours, even their smell would send your mind back to its abstractions and convoluted reveries. At least that's what I would have said if he'd let me finish but he was leaning out of his seat and yelling at me, 'Don't contradict me in my own house.'

Very well, I decided, I won't.

Candour

Barney's language carried traces of older ways of speaking which may have been from Irish or Scots, or expressions that were coined in the country, perhaps just out of the imagination of someone struggling for a word not to be reached.

One of his words was 'gulpin'. A gulpin is a fool. A dictionary of Scots says 'gelpin' is a variant of it and describes a stoutly built young fellow.

'Ach, what would you listen to that gulpin for?'

And as I have learned it from him, a gulpin was a specific kind of fool, a village idiot, someone lacking in basic sense or an easy grasp of the mores of the local society. A gulpin got simple things wrong. He – I never heard Barney call a woman a gulpin – might have great intelligence, be good at counting or fixing engines. But he would not know what was expected of him by his neighbours.

'That gulpin doesn't know his arse from his elbow.'

One gulpin was a man who passed the plate at church. This puzzled me. Surely this was a man who was respected by his neighbours and the priest, who was trusted with money and given a position of responsibility.

His duties included monitoring the behaviour of children in the pews, even calling them out to the end of the pew, away from their friends, if they were noisy or fidgety.

'What does that gulpin know about anything?'

In Barney's view this man had made himself ridiculous through the self-importance that had allowed him to police the church, as if he was better than the rest of us. Only a gulpin would have failed to see that his neighbours would mock him for putting himself over them.

Yet a gulpin was not necessarily a contemptible idiot, just one with clumsy manners. The sort of man who'd make a hames of anything.

Another class of idiot was the lig.

A child who was distracted and mischievous would be told to 'stop acting the lig'. To act the lig was to be giddy or silly, a playful fool. A similar expression is 'acting the maggot'. But we know what the maggot is: I have no idea what an actual lig is. I suppose it was a class of lunatic or deranged person, beyond our powers to fully emulate, since we were always taken for playing the role.

Barney had a gift for derision and when he referred to someone as 'that lig', the hard 'g', as in gulpin, made him sound almost as if he was clearing his throat of the bad taste that person put there. But even words like gulpin and lig, the way he used them, implied some affection which could not be suggested by calling someone a plain fool.

A man might be called an eejit, as distinct from an idiot; the eejit again presenting a simulation of stupidity, while the idiot was merely contemptible. These words attributed our stupidity to wilfulness, not to innate deficiency. Barney's generation passed a moral judgement on most slow-wittedness it encountered. Harsher terms were reserved for real dullness of mind.

I wonder if this thinking came from the teachers he had had and their own much larger lexicon of contempt.

A word with real affection in it was 'cutty'.

Barney would come into the living room, find me sitting in his chair, and he would pat me on the back of the head and say, 'come on, cutty.'

He was evicting me from his seat, but nicely.

A cutty, as he used the word, might be a boy or a girl, though if a boy, only a small boy or a boy in the family.

If he had said, 'you know that wee cutty in the shop?' you would know that he was talking about a girl.

The nearest normal English word to 'cutty' is 'darling' but 'cutty' is, if anything, not a substitute for 'darling' but an evasion of it. Barney would never have used a word as frankly loving as 'darling'. The word 'cutty' allowed him a detachment from the person addressed. We used the words Ma and Da in the same way, as evasions of mummy and daddy, when we wanted to be a little tougher.

He would also call me Charlie, and then I understood that he was being more assertive, even aggressive. 'Come on, Charlie, shift!'

If he said that someone was 'a right Charlie', this meant plainly that he was a fool, a gulpin.

And worse than a Charlie was a hallion, for now we were outside the range of good-humoured interest altogether. A hallion was a contemptible layabout or messer.

What strikes me now about many of Barney's words is that they were evasions of specific thought.

He would say, 'would you take a look at the cut of that hallion,' leaving it to you to work out for yourself what was wrong with his attire or grooming.

'Give me a lock – or a rake – of them yokes.'

It seemed important not to be precise when dealing with quantity or number. He would take a lock, not five or ten.

'Hand me that yoke there,' he might say, waving his hand out impatiently, the real name of the thing being of no interest to him.

'What?'

'That yoke.'

And you would feel that you had failed to properly accord with him, to think and comprehend like him. You would know that other boys would understand immediately what yoke he was talking about.

'Och, can you do nothing right? The spanner. It's called a spanner.' As if it was you who had failed to name it.

But the objects that were described by these words were not complicated things that presented any challenge to his powers of conception. They were just yokes, things that you used every day.

A book wouldn't have been a yoke. A yoke is never complicated. A television would never have been a yoke. A yoke was nearly always a tool.

His adjectives were as nebulous. He really only had one or two, but the inflection let you know whether or not they were meant ironically. 'Quare', as in 'thon's a quare yoke', was an Irish pronunciation of queer, perhaps initially, but Barney used it as a different word altogether. 'That's a quare day' meaning 'that's a lovely day', not a queer day, though perhaps an unusual day.

The word was often entirely affirmative.

Or 'that's quare rain'. Meaning 'that's wild rain', which is not the same as savage or heartless rain. 'Wild' meaning much the same as 'quare'. Something was wild or quare if it was to be wondered at.

Barney might have described a man as 'wild civil' or 'quare and civil'. These expressions meant that the man's manners were impressive and remarkable.

But these weren't words that told you a lot about the character of the things they described. Saying, 'he's a quare gulpin' told you nothing about what species of gulpin he was, only that his being a gulpin was something to be marvelled at.

Other collective nouns were 'clatter' and 'shower'. 'Clatter' for children, as in 'a clatter of weans', 'shower' for people he didn't like, as in 'that shower of hallions' or 'that shower'. These were words which averted the need to count, or even to say exactly what it was you thought of the people you described by them.

You might hear him talk of people as 'beings', as in 'I don't know what class of being he thinks he is.'

Barney lived in a world in which spanners and knives and even people were not named. The yoke and the cutty and the gulpin were to be spoken of a little coyly, in case others listening in should know what you were talking about.

There were other traditional language terms used around me growing up, like 'thran', to describe a grumpy person of few words and dry humour. Barney never used those other words much. The beauty of those words is in their capacity to sharpen thought and refine an image. Barney was not preserving an old language so much as an old code.

He discouraged any kind of candour. I think he saw himself as a wary, solitary hero in the story of his own life. Holding on to information about yourself made as much sense as holding on to your money. The world was a dangerous place to be negotiated with care, not just because some people were devious but because many were stupid. Part with a little fact about your doings, and there was no knowing where it would end up or how it might embarrass you.

My mother had secrets too. Having lived through the Blitz, nursing wounded soldiers in London, she rarely talked about it. The only thing I know about her training days, for instance, is that she collected owls or something, and that a student coming in the window after hours had knocked them over and smashed a lot of them and put her off collecting any more.

I wonder if Barney had had a painful experience arising from undue care with gossip. Maybe he had let go of a secret and it had travelled to those who would be most appalled or gladdened by it.

You could have understood if his caution had applied only to practical, business secrets. Barney, behind the bar, saw a lot of fixers and chancers. Maybe one would offer him a cheap sale; another needed information to complete a deal. Or maybe a barman, confided with too much information about the criminal or amorous antics of customers, simply learnt to pass none of it on, never to be the one who could be blamed when the police or a slighted woman called in.

He often scolded me for candour – 'What did you tell him that for? What business is it of his? How many times do you have to be told?

Trust no one. Sure, what does that clown/fool/gulpin know about anything?'

Maybe this caution was just a part of the rural culture, a ground rule for survival in a border county with a history of smuggling, violent activism, secret societies and hayshed sex.

As small children this economy with information was imbued into us through nursery rhymes:

> *Tell tale tit,*
> *your ma can't knit.*
> *Your granny cannae go to bed*
> *without a dummy tit.*

If you don't know to keep your mouth shut, you know nothing. Talking too frankly disgraces your family and betrays generations before you. The blabbermouth comes of bad stock.

In such a culture you 'ask no questions' because 'what you don't know can't hurt you.' Barney embodied those values, or tried to, and sought to impart them, hopelessly, to his gregarious children.

He would pick us up from school occasionally, sit quietly driving us to the barber, saying nothing about where we were going, leaving us wondering if he was taking us on a long journey or planning to kill us and bury us somewhere.

Once he took me 'for a drive' on a Sunday afternoon – ostensibly for pleasure. Then we went home and sat with the rest of the family watching television, and said nothing about where we'd been. We had gone to a scrapyard on the side of Black Mountain. I had stood rubbing my hands together, my legs chilled, waiting for him to finish negotiating a price for an engine part for his car. We were surrounded by heaps of broken and scrapped motors and, in my raw exposed state their edges had seemed to grate my skin if I stood close to them. Barney didn't feel obliged to hurry things along for my sake. This was man's stuff.

I was, I understood, to say nothing about it to anyone.

Other fathers initiated sons into manhood by taking them to football matches or the pub; mine initiated me by trying to teach me the habit of secrecy.

Those who seek celebrity by telling their life stories, would have been ridiculous to him. If your worth was measured, as for him it was, by how much of yourself you could keep to yourself, then these yaps were demeaning themselves as much as if they were flaunting their naked bodies in the street or handing out cash to strangers.

He conducted himself like a criminal. He made transactions in whispers. If you asked him where the best place was to buy brake fluid or four-ply he'd say, 'who wants to know?'

In his world, you went to the front door of a house to talk to the woman and round the back to talk to the man.

He would have thought that those who flaunted private information about themselves had simply failed to understand how to live life practically and with due caution.

And yet, when Barney was drunk he was voluble. He would not be talked over by anyone, least of all by an upstart son. He would have his say.

But this extravagance was always of opinion rather than information. Details, facts; these he instinctively preserved, even in his cups. Challenge him when he was in a sweeter mood and the reply would be, 'I know what I know' or, 'don't talk to me about so-and-so. There's nothing you can tell me about him. He knows nothing about anything.'

And whether Barney knew much at all can not now be told, for he kept it all to himself.

Dirt

We were dirty back then. What else would you expect when we were so cold? It was normal to shiver in bed before your own body would impart heat to the sheets. And water was cold unless you stoked up a fire and pulled the damper out to get the boiler going or turned on the immersion heater – if you had one – and that cost money.

There were eight of us living in a house with two-and-a-half bedrooms and one toilet. If we had lived by today's standards, the demand on heat and toilet paper would have been unsustainable. So we were cold and didn't wash much and wiped our bottoms with *The Irish News*, which meant that we were dirtier still, since newsprint is not an efficient cleaner of any surface, except perhaps glass.

We did not know we were dirty. The black rim of the fingernails was just normal.

There was a television advertisement at the time selling toothpaste; 'You'll wonder where the yellow went, when you brush your teeth with Pepsodent.' The understanding of the creators was that having clean white teeth would be a new experience for most viewers.

There was also evidence of the normality of dirt in the humour of teenage boys, getting used to the clamminess of puberty. They would joke about clinkers and cheese, the matting of hair like rough brier across an untended gateway, the excretions from the glans.

These were among the normal discomforts of being physical – original sin perhaps – like waking in the mornings with a gummed-up eye, or a flea – actual, not metaphorical – in the ear, and the hideous intimate noise of its struggle, or the biting of the nails and the occasional tearing of the skin beside them through over-enthusiasm.

Neither of my parents had teeth. Barney told me that they had gone together to get them all out when the National Health Service came in and they had drunk a half bottle of whiskey together afterwards. Before that, toothache had often been treated with potassium nitrate. Bad teeth were pulled out with pliers. There were stories of people tying one end of a length of string around a tooth and the other end to a door handle. I can't imagine a conclusion to the process that would have achieved much.

But when I was a child there were many grown-ups who had only gums to chew with and kept their gnashers in a glass by the bed while they slept. A man might amuse his children by nudging his dentures out, presumably with his tongue, and clenching them with his raw gums, to suggest a hungry skeletal appendage escaping his face.

And it may be because we were expected in time to lose our own teeth too that tooth care was lax.

No one seriously expected us to stop eating sweets. If that suggestion was made in television advertisements or by the dentist, then that could be dismissed as more government advice that no ordinary person needed to take seriously.

Indeed, once when I was hungry and there was nothing much in the house, Barney gave me a sugar sandwich. I liked sugar sandwiches. The grit of sugar and the pastiness of bread, mediated by the slime of margarine was interesting in a wholly tactile and unexpected way.

There were no paper tissues yet, so mothers provided their children with clean cotton hankies when sending them out to Mass. By Wednesday, they would be dangerous to have about you.

Occasionally my mother would throw a fit over the smell of feet from under the dinner table and firm resolutions would be made, but nothing much changed from year to year.

Barney was from Donegal where nobody washed because it was even colder there. I visited a cottage in the 1980s and saw that the shower unit was where they threw their shoes. The man of the house explained that he had had the shower and inside toilet installed 'on a grant'.

There were two boys living at the end of our street, who were talked about for being clean. Brendan and Paul shone. They were sent out to play in bright beautiful jumpers and white socks, with their hair combed, which is not how you equipped a child for the fields and building sites round an expanding urban development.

I heard my mother marvel at how clean Brendan and Paul were, or more precisely, at the trouble their mother had taken to turn them out so nicely, virtually ornamentally.

She could honestly share that wonder with other parents who took little more trouble over their children's weekday appearance than she did herself.

And once, on a blowy day, when Brendan was whisked over into the mud and ran crying home, we all felt this was a far greater calamity than immersion in mud would have been for any of the rest of us.

We, as children, leapt streams and splashed muck over ourselves and would get into trouble for coming home excessively dirty, but there seems to have been a normal level of griminess that ordinary rough-and-tumble could not significantly worsen. And it would not get you into major trouble.

This just means that we were poor and didn't notice it. There was cultural acceptance of what would now be called dirt but which we didn't think of as dirt at all. For we knew people who really were dirty and we were not allowed to play with their children, children who were actually blackened by the filth they lived in.

We had a bath night, though it was a flexible arrangement and probably slipped past for weeks at a time. At the start of each day I washed my face at the bathroom sink, when I could get in for long enough.

Sometimes my interest in washing was enlivened by the discomfort of being dirty.

For want of much warm water getting into my ears, they would fill with hard wax that I could pick out with a needle. But the wax was awkwardly placed. I could not pick at it without pushing it further in. Then I would get neuralgia and be sent to the doctor to be syringed. For a child, the slosh of warm liquid inside a clean ear is the most thrilling physical sensation.

Barney? Did he wash? In films about working-class life, the father is often depicted at the kitchen sink soaping his body, or shedding the grime of his exertions into a hot tub, usually in front of the fire, though we always had a bathroom.

I have no images to recall of Barney in the bath. If he had been working at the car on a Sunday afternoon, he would rub his hands and forearms with Swarfega and change his shirt.

I recall the shudder and blurt of his splashing cold water over his face, but this was perhaps more to refresh than to clean himself.

He smelt of alcohol and tobacco, of wet wool and sweat, of old leather and new polish. His hands were stained with oil and nicotine. All this was, to my eye, normal in a man; it was what he should smell like; it was a fragrance he would do well to replicate if he was afraid others might think he had gone soft.

Trace elements of sauce and vinegar, wiped from the mouth with a cuff; old cotton that was farted through a thousand times since those trousers were last washed; wood smoke, tobacco and turf smoke; excretions, some redolent of the earth, some of the sea.

Barney just exuded the impress of his life.

Connoisseurs of fragrance and taste, who discuss wine and whiskey or bottled scent, find vanilla in Cotes du Rhone, leather in Talisker or diesel oil in Bushmills.

The wax picked from the ear on the tip of a car key, or the grime under Barney's thumbnail, might have matured for as long.

The only perfume on his body was soap. Because he shaved, we often bought him Old Spice for Christmas. And he would smell a little chastened for a time.

The older smells of the bar he worked in included stale cigarette smoke and beer, carbolic and a disinfectant, even burnt newspaper. When meths drinkers use the toilets, he told me, the smoke clears the stench.

But old and damp newspaper has its own must that accumulates in the pocket. So do pencils and watch straps and even coins. The smell of Barney settled in the end into a flat staleness that belied the variety of its ingredients.

Noises

There is a polite way to sneeze. It is probably dangerous. You clench everything and contain the burst, which means that it probably fires back into your brain. It sounds like: Hing! You often see men do it in public places. They push a knuckle in to the upper lip to dull the reflex and then they spasm girlishly. Hing!

Barney wasn't a Hing! man. His sneeze was loud and uninhibited. It was the sneeze of a man who had passed his early years in open fields and close to animals. It was an animal noise. Men probably sneezed like this fifty thousand years ago, lavishly, unselfconsciously and – primarily – efficiently; for a loud sneeze such as nature intends sends a shudder through the whole body and, apart from clearing the sinuses, probably does a lot of good for the liver and kidneys too.

It was not just in his sneezing that Barney was natural and animalistic.

He stretched like an old dog when he was tired. I often saw him bunch his shoulders and stretch his arms out above him, presumably to stimulate the circulation for a little extra energy. But he would enliven his lungs too, not with a yawn, but with a loud, 'Oh Hay Ho!' The wording never varied. This vocalised stretch signalled to every part of his body that it was time to relax its readiness for work or a quarrel. It was the kind of general 'at ease' to all the forces of nervous attentiveness.

I'm sure both anthropology and biology could have benefited from a scan of Barney's body when he stretched, for we would have learnt from him how the pre-Neolithic beast man settled himself by the evening fire and we would have seen reactions in the behaviour of all his organs.

But why was it so loud and so specific? Was it a signal to the rest of the group that the primal man-beast, for now, offered no threat? I think that is how we, his children, naturally read it. The ardent attention of the worrying man had been switched off, disengaged, as methodically as a rifle is unloaded or a bowstring detached.

There were other times with Barney when nature was working in him, without him being aware of it, making of him a creature that he had no notion of being.

Like when he picked his nose in a wholly abstracted state. He would look for a moment at the produce on his finger, as bewildered as an ape, before coming back to himself and flicking it dismissively into the fire. We all displace instincts, say psychologists. When you suppress one impulse – perhaps to speak – another takes its place. You might run your hand over your head in a grooming movement. Barney had lots of these little grooming gestures, but I don't know if they suggested other instincts stifled or what those other instincts might have been.

He often clasped his own jawbone with his hand, rubbing hard against the bristle of his cheeks with his fingers and thumb, as if testing the texture or the firmness of the bone.

And he sat in an armchair, almost crouching, as if ready to reach for something. He would rest his elbows on his knees and clasp his hands, rubbing the heels of them together the way some men would when they crushed tobacco.

Maybe he should have been whittling a stick.

When he was in hospital with the DTs near the end of his life, he sat up in bed with the sheet in his hands and twisted it as if he thought he was making a rope.

73

All his life he was restless to be kneading or twisting or snapping or moulding in instinctive hands which remembered denial.

When we were lazing around as children on summer holidays he would snap: 'would you ever get out from under my feet and do something.'

Then he would sit and crouch forward, elbows on his knees, hands clasped, ready.

Drinking

Barney boasted that he never had a hangover. My own experience was that the hangover made heavy drinking untenable, especially after about the age of thirty. I suspect Barney lived with a perpetual hangover; that it was his normality. There was an easy cure for the discomfort, another drink.

In later years he was plainly frank about this. After the funeral of his brother Michael, there was talk of going to the pub, just for one. He was red in the face and shifting on his seat, desperate. When I made sure he didn't get his fix, he was furious and sullen. He could see only malice in what I had done, as if I had deprived him of aspirin for a headache and wanted him to suffer.

He was, at this stage, immersed in the ecology of alcoholism. Life was patterned around the routine need.

One day I called an ambulance for him because he was coughing up blood. I had found him sitting on his bed, unable to walk downstairs or stand for long without falling over. He had a whiskey in one hand and a plastic bag in the other to catch the thick red gunk from his throat. Where, he asked, would he get a drink when he was in hospital? Would I bring him one?

He refused to acknowledge the connection between the bleeding and the whiskey, except for the need to cough more blood up to help get the whiskey down.

This wasn't stupidity. It was acceptance of the simple need for whiskey, whether it killed him or not. The failure to see that, was not in him but in me. That's why he took me for a fool or judged me perverse.

He had that knowing eye you see on street winos, who sneer back at us if we betray any contempt or even curiosity. They know it all themselves already.

Are you going to moralise? They have heard it before, and found that it did not help.

Social Drinking

Barney died without getting his head round why some people went into pubs and bought water. He had long assumed that many people in this world are plain stupid. One of his favourite expressions was, 'did you ever see the like of that?' He sneered at people who behaved, by his terms, oddly. He marvelled at ignorance, and yet he was always open to being further surprised by the unplumbed depths of unreflecting minds. He came out of a culture which was profoundly concerned with appearance. He would never have been able to sit drinking a glass of water in a pub without fearing that someone from 1930s Donegal was watching him and saying, 'did you ever see the like of that?'

If you wanted water, there was plenty in the tap at home. And he also sneered at people who came into pubs and sat over one drink for two hours.

Drink was business. Those who hogged a seat and had only one drink were keeping that seat from others who would have sat happily all day and lashed copious pints into themselves, thereby feeding the till.

And while he may have merely chuckled bemusedly (on a good day) at those who paid money for water, he would have had nothing but admiration for the cynical entrepreneurs who had discovered that water could be sold.

Apart from his business head, Barney had a different affection for pubs, one that probably rivalled his business sense, even hindered it.

He was a drinker and he loved the pub culture. He felt that a man was virtually defined by his place in that culture. The pub had its rules and Barney, having worked in bars, and drunk in bars for decades, knew well what manner of conduct was expected of him. A real man was at home in a pub and entered into its mores enthusiastically. He drank plenty and he bought drinks for others. He competed for the right to buy a round but he knew when he was entitled to lose. A man who didn't succeed in winning the right to buy his round, when it was his turn, was beneath contempt.

When I worked with him in my teens I got a hint of his grasp on life. He could recognise that Joe or Rusty was 'a real man' – which was different from 'a hard man'. But your man over there was 'just a mouth'. I couldn't have told the difference.

He often saw my civilities towards people in bars as misplaced. When I liked someone, he routinely told me that the man was a 'user' or a 'waste of space'.

I never discerned the rules by which he assessed people. He would have had me believe that he trusted virtually nobody, and yet in bars he always had friends.

He saw the world as a desert full of pub oases in which he could refresh himself. On the drive to Dublin for his brother's funeral twenty years ago, he pointed out practically every pub on the old road as one he had stopped at and met some character in – in which he had not been allowed to put his hand in his pocket. Then he told this story.

'One day the guards came along and saw you all in the car, drinking minerals and eating crisps. And one of them asked Ann where your mum and dad were. And she said "Mammy and Daddy are in the pub having a drink." And the guard said, "that's all right then" and went on his way.'

And Barney's reflective, even nostalgic, summing up was: 'that wouldn't happen today.'

This had been a better country, to his mind, when the police left you alone. Barney understood that there were sensible rules governing even such things as parenting and drinking. He also believed that rules should be flexible, and one of the things they should flex most tolerantly around was a working man's need for a drink.

The Pub

Drunkenness in Barney's day was predominantly a working man's pleasure. If you opened the door of a pub in 1965 and looked in, you would see men solemnly drinking at the bar in their cloth caps. Drinking was more physical then and went more to the stomach than to the head. Regular drinkers got fat. Men had beer bellies. You knew they were drunk because they farted, burped and slurred words, not because they were leaping up and down and yelling at each other. Drink relaxed a man at the end of a working day, though there would always be one or two in a bar who had been there since morning. It was not loud nor part of the mating game.

I worked in bars myself when there was a clear distinction between the public bar and the lounge. The public bar was for men. You could spit on the floor in some of the dingier ones. The toilets were just a flaky wall and a cubicle that was so foul only a desperate man would use it.

Women might come in to the bar occasionally. I never, except in England, saw a bar that excluded women. Children would pass through, selling the evening paper. These might be indulged; beggars weren't. The television would be on but softly. If the customer wanted to pay special attention, he'd ask Barney to turn it up for a few minutes. There was never music in a public bar then.

The lounge was always a cleaner more comfortable area. You could bring your wife or girlfriend in, but in those days, it was not a place you'd have gone to in hopes of meeting a woman.

The dour and solemn public bar was a place in which a barman needed to develop skills. The old porter barrels were complicated. There would be four or five of them in a row on a rough plank shelf. There was a tap in the side of them and a bung that could be released to ease the pressure or retained to keep it, depending on whether you wanted the black of the stout, or the high white. Sometimes they would splutter. It might take several minutes to pour a pint, and this would involve scooping out excess white with a plastic blade, and running that blade across the top of the glass to scrape off the sloppier mess, and spread the surface evenly. Porter was the cheapest pint in the bar and the most trouble, which tells you how highly a barman's labour was valued.

The barman had to do more than serve drink. He had to monitor the floor to be sure that there were no messers in. He had to deal with fights, brush up around the customers and wipe the bar and the tables. He had also to endure the tedium of slurred but ardent conversation and extract himself promptly, without giving offence. Barney was valued for all these skills.

The almost church-like hush of the public bar was overwhelmed on Saturday afternoons. There was a pulse, a rhythm, to life in the pub then, dictated by the times of races. The customers flowed back and forth to the bookies nearby, placing their bets then dashing to watch the race and gulp a drink. The more concerted gambler would often skip the drink, and the flush winner might clear off as soon as the bet was cashed, to avoid having to buy a large round: so this symbiotic relationship between the pub and the bookie didn't always deliver the cash it promised.

Look in during a race and the floor would be heaving with life. A moment later it would be empty and the usual litter of ash and butts would be further embellished with torn betting slips.

I used to enjoy the carnival of drinking and betting and get absorbed into the group mood for the duration of the race. Then, instantly it was over, they would rush to the bar for a drink and I would need to work. Serving men in a bar entailed a repeated shifting between identifying with them and detaching from them.

The tactful barman needed to exercise care at such trying times for his customers, not to break a man's concentration by asking him to clarify an order while the runners were hot and frantic, or to make some glib remark to a punter when he was angry at his losses.

The frustration for a publican was that all this fretting about horses might not sell enough drink. It would also bring people into the bar who were not regulars but whose brasher manners might disturb those who had come to think of the pub as home. So people who were happy to buy drink might be ousted by others who took better care of their cash.

But this was an insight into working men at play. Where would they go when the races ended and they had drunk their fill? Home, to report to wives how much money they had spent?

The security of the old pubs was in the dependability of the regulars and in the hierarchical pecking order among men drinking, like jungle beasts at their pool.

In the public bar then, men were at their most sexless. They were dirty and unshaven. Their rough clothes didn't fit well. They were beery and fat and they had bad teeth. A man was as free to be a slob there as in his own home, indeed more free. Many preferred the pub to their own living room. A man might approach his wife and his boss in the same tentative spirit, for these were people to whom he would have to explain himself. In the pub, he could relax and fart. One who was well groomed among them would attract attention, even suspicion, and obviously had other intentions than to simply join in.

I don't know if Barney was drunk much as a young man. As the father of a young family, he did not seem to be drunk often, but I would not have noticed. He was moody, which may mean he was governed by hangovers and thirsts. But it was in his old age that he turned into a repulsive drinker, slobbering and demeaned by it, much as if it was an accessory of ageing, combining with the natural depletion of his body, to pull him down. When he ate, his mouth reached out for the fork, wary of bringing the fork to the mouth and missing.

Still, he lived to the age of eighty-seven, having smoked and drunk all his life.

Language

Barney knew the need to be careful with language. As a barman he knew the sensitivities that were easily needled. He wouldn't have wanted any chatter about homos, queens or queers; at least not when Vincey was about. Vincey was my first full-blown gay acquaintance, a man whose extravagant posturing struck me as caricature but never changed. This was how he really was, the limp wrist and the wee shuffle.

The policing of language in Barney's bar was mostly out of consideration for those in present company who would be offended. Later, if you talked about Vincey and his marvellous mannerisms, the terms used would be the common ones, not the ornate modern contrivances. 'He's a homo because he's a homo. How would I know?'

If you'd said, 'don't say homo, say gay,' Barney would have laughed at you. But there were words which were extreme then, which he would not have allowed a child to use. 'The proper word is Negro,' he would explain.

And he had a coy way of avoiding the words Catholic and Protestant. He said 'your own' and 'the other sort'.

This was perhaps out of a sense that denominational labels didn't fully describe what divided people. Or maybe it was out of deference to those religious terms, which should not just be marks of difference. Or maybe it was because the term Protestant, as deployed by sectarian Catholics, had been elided into 'Prod'. To use it that way would be to let himself down. He wouldn't want to be thought a bigot. And to say the full word Protestant would come across as an affectation. So Protestants were always just 'the other sort'.

To describe himself as a Catholic would be to assert religious faith, and to describe a political position as Catholic would be simply inaccurate.

Once, in the bar, I called out an order for 'two Monks by the neck'. That annoyed him and he thought I had stupidly allowed myself to be set up. If you already had a glass for your drink in a public bar, you ordered only a bottle – 'by the neck'. No harm was done when the order was for a Double Diamond or a Blue Bass. The worst they could be mistaken for was a piece of jewellery or a sick fish.

And this was a line he had heard before. I had heard it myself. In truth, I had been waiting for an opportunity to use it. Catholic barmen in Belfast perhaps imagined that sales of Monk ale were soaring in Protestant areas, just on the back of enthusiasm for that joke.

In a bar, there are always other people listening who might take malicious relish in repeating words by which men have made fools of themselves, even words spoken with affection.

People in those days were nearly all given pejorative nicknames: Shorty, Sniffy, Blackie. These were comments on physical appearance, or they were elisions of real names, like Barney for Bernard. They all expressed a presumption of familiarity and intrusion. And it was stuffy or sniffy to refuse your nickname and deny people their link to your private self.

Look back into Irish mythology and you find the same thing there, people being identified by their physical attributes or handicaps, Lugh of the Long Arms, Balor of the evil eye, Fionn MacCumhal, named after his fair hair, Maol – or Baldy. Barney was never Barney at home. My mother and his sister, in the end, were the only people in the world who called him Bernard.

In Barney's world, being nameable meant allowing yourself to belong. Denying people the right to this hold on you, their right to name you, was self-importance and distance. It implied that you were not fully in their society, not one of the boys.

An insistence on propriety and proper names removed you from the humour – often cruel – of other men. You paid with your name for the privilege of being inside, and yourself free to offend others.

That power becomes more obvious when it is assumed too freely, as by the English barman who addresses you as Paddy. 'What can I do for you, Paddy?'

He'll not say it again.

The world in which Barney moved was full of awkward language. Whenever I sat in the bar after work with the other staff, taking a drink and unwinding, language was frequently checked. There always, in my memory of these sessions, seems to have been an older wiser man present, gently policing the terms used; ticking off someone for swearing in front of me, the boy, or talking about politics in front of a Protestant or sex in front of a woman, or work secrets in front of the boss.

But you couldn't actually offend someone who wasn't there. There was no word in those days that could have got Barney sacked unless directed against a real and present person. Then, it would not necessarily have had to be a very bad word. All that would have mattered would have been the offence taken. And people then decided for themselves how offended they would like to be.

Jokes

I can only remember one joke that my father ever told me. 'Did you hear about the sexy crow? ... He was raven mad.'

Barney thought this was hilarious.

'But,' I probably said, 'a crow doesn't mate with a raven.'

'Isn't a raven a crow?' a brother would ask. And then someone would check the dictionary. And Barney's joke would be in pieces on the floor. He had only been trying to make his sons laugh. He had only wanted them to see his funny side.

Sexy crow? Raven mad? He and the men in the pub had probably laughed till it hurt when they heard that one, or at least for as long as a drinker will keep his mouth open without remembering to pour something into it.

What surprises me about the sexy crow joke, when I reflect on it now, is how innocent it was. There was no cruelty in it and no real bawdiness either. It could just as easily have been: did you hear about the paranoid crow? In fact, if it had been, we probably would have laughed. 'Paranoia' was one of those deep words that sixth formers played with: 'just because you're paranoid doesn't mean they're not out to get you.'

There was a whole series of sexy something jokes then. The sexy coalman: he dropped his bags down an entry. I didn't really get that one but Barney just snorted when I tried it out on him as a belated attempt to share his kind of humour. It was too raw to share with children and he'd probably heard it already.

The sexy crow joke had confused us for more than its ornithological inexactitude. It wasn't Barney's usual kind of joke. Bawdy riddles were out of line with his genius, which was for the humour of deadpan exaggeration, telling ridiculous tales with a straight face and then laughing when a child has been persuaded to believe them.

He had told us that thunder was caused by clouds bumping together and he never bothered to correct us. He didn't need us to acknowledge that we had been fooled. He was self sufficient in his humour, able to enjoy it alone.

Barney wasn't really a joke teller but he was a jocund man. He was a conversational drinker. In the pub he was laughing all the time, mocking and scoffing. None of this could be packaged and taken home. It wasn't set piece performances; it was interaction. I can do the same thing myself and have, presumably, inherited the tendency from him. I dread to think how much else of me I may have inherited from him.

Barney believed he had dependable standards in humour. Tony Hancock and Harry Worth were funny. Ken Dodd was just ridiculous, which was funny in a way; you can laugh at the ridiculous. But how could you laugh at Monty Python?

'Och, you're easy amused,' he would say, as if he thought resilience against being amused was a mark of maturity.

What he hated about Monty Python was the agreement among his children that it was funny, when it plainly wasn't. He thought we had succumbed to a generational onus to enjoy absurdity and pretension. It was all a con on people like him, contrived to make them feel obsolete. It was like a coded language devised by teenagers to exclude their parents.

Well, if the joke was on him, he wasn't having it.

'Catch yourselves on, laughing at that nonsense.'

You couldn't tell him what was funny and what was not. Hattie Jacques working as a bus conductor was funny. Tony Hancock finding an unexploded bomb in his garden was funny. Dead parrot? Sure anyone can see that it's dead. Calling it an 'ex-parrot' doesn't advance the narrative, it just indulges the moment.

Barney should have recognised that as clowning, for he had loved the circus. Chipperfield's Circus would come every year and Barney would take his wee boys to marvel, but we were small and intimidated by the shouts of the ringmaster and the horrors befalling the poor clowns, tripping over, their car collapsing in bits, the bangs, the pathetic inevitability of nothing working for them, the mystery of this being funny. I didn't find it funny.

I didn't want the lion tamer to go into the cage, yet when he started cracking his long whip, I felt that he deserved to get his head bitten off. The poor boxing kangaroos surely didn't want to be punched on their noses, but Barney would explain that they enjoyed it.

The circus comes back to me as a disappointment because Barney had built up my expectations of the magic of it and had tried to appeal to a child's fantasy.

Or the posters had perhaps seemed magical and light, conveying nothing of the musty smell, the damp straw and the rough scary men in charge. It struck me as a stratagem by poor and unhappy people to make money by pretending to be happy and charming, and getting it wrong. That was the five-year-old's take on it anyway, or the adult mind's interpretation of the remembered awfulness of it.

Someone – perhaps Barney – said that the boxing kangaroo was a southpaw. He had a glass jaw. This compounded my worries.

Others might have marvelled at the actual strength and dexterity of the high trapeze artists but to my mind we were only there to see if they would fall or not. I only fretted for them, and I was relieved when they came down.

And I didn't understand the bareback riders, since it was plain that their backs were not bare at all, and that, in terms of the challenge to stand on a running horse, it made little obvious difference whether you had a shirt on or not.

When I was older I thought Barney's humour and mine had converged.

I took him to see Dave Allen one night at the Grand Opera House in Belfast, thinking he would love the show. He didn't. Allen had cursed and sworn on stage as much as Barney himself would have done in the bar.

Barney said, 'Every fucking second word was fuck. He's a fucking disgrace.'

Music

Music told Barney that the world was deteriorating.

There had been an age, which he had known, when people sang clearly and to the point, but now singers mumbled and shrieked; you usually couldn't make out the words and these didn't make much sense when you could.

He had loved Harry Belafonte and Kenneth McKellar. He could not sit quietly through *Top of the Pops*, even in the fairly tame 1960s, the age of wholesome bands like Herman's Hermits and Jerry and the Pacemakers.

'He's singing through his nose.'

He saw the Rolling Stones as an aberration.

Jimi Hendrix? Well now you were not even being serious.

We were six children who had come between 1948 and 1956, so we were all teenagers in the late 1960s and well beyond his reach. None of us looked up to him and he felt the loss.

The generational war over music in the rest of the country was a fascinating cultural tension by which that era is remembered. In our house it was more serious than that.

On Thursday evening we would sit around the telly to be engrossed by Procul Harum or Dusty Springfield or The Four Tops, all the time begrudging the little attention that we had to give to listening for his key in the door.

Then someone would jump up and turn the sound down. But still he would walk into a living room of hushed children, his whole family uncharacteristically united and focused, and he would say, before anything else: 'Get that bloody racket off. What sort of noise is that for a man to come home to?'

He had picked up correctly on the spirit of the music we loved. Some of it was intended as an affront to an older generation's mores and loves. It offered us a way of growing up differently from him.

His own youthful rebellion against childhood had set him out early towards being a man. His way of pretending to be grown up back in the 1920s had been to model himself on the generation that preceded him. Our way was to adopt wholly different tastes from his. Well, what was that if not rejection?

But much of our music was just about love and jauntiness. We did like Harry Belafonte. 'There is a hole in the bucket, dear Liza, dear Liza ...'

We would sing along with that, priding ourselves on remembering the next obstacle to repairing that hole, anticipating the completion of the cycle.

And Barney would concede that he liked Dusty Springfield or Petula Clark. At least Dusty Springfield was modest, he observed. She didn't have her skirt up around her arse. This, by his view, was a credit to her.

He hadn't the resources to notice – nor had I – that Dusty was a lesbian. She was simply a good modest woman at a time when trollops like Marianne Faithfull were on the news, scandalising the world.

The bigger worry still for Barney was the nancy boys. There was a period from the mid-1960s when men seemed to want to be women. They wore long hair that was smooth and groomed. Some of these men were not gay at all. And they were not deliberate gender benders, like Bowie, clowning with their sexuality. They were not challenging us to rethink anything; this was just their way of countering the aggressive image of manhood, inherited from the war.

Occasionally, say on a Sunday evening, when Mum was present too, during *Sunday Night at the London Palladium*, we could have a discussion about music.

'Just listen and you might like it.' Kenneth McKellar would be singing 'A Man Without Love' or 'Flow Gently Sweet Afton'. And of course, we would talk over it and annoy him, not realising that this voice and this song were replete with nostalgic resonances for him. We only knew Sweet Afton as a brand of cigarettes. We only ever expected music to separate us from him, to reassure us of the value of our distance from him. His liking a piece of music was reason enough for us not to.

Photography

Barney didn't have a lot of photographs. I never saw his wedding album, if he had one. He had no family photographs hung about the house. I have never seen a picture of his mother and father or most of his wider family. When I reflect on this now, I wonder if I have stumbled on old evidence of a great secret.

I have no photographs of my mother from her youth or working life in London.

Once Barney dug out for me a single photograph of his wedding to settle an argument his sister had raised. She had complained in her nineties, that their parents had boycotted her wedding. Barney brought out a picture to show that his parents had not been at his wedding either. His point was that this was no big deal; they just didn't go to weddings.

In fact, he didn't come to mine.

Yet there was another face in the picture that I recognized. It was that of the Nationalist Party leader, Eddie McAteer. He had featured on the news often when I was young.

Why had Barney never remarked, back then, that he had known him?

Photographs? They catch a moment in time, a fraction of a second, and make that moment meaningful for decades, even progressively more meaningful with the passing years.

Maybe Eddie McAteer just happened to be in the hotel that day and thought it good electioneering to put himself about, even to the extent of swelling a modest wedding party. Or maybe Barney had a political life he never spoke of. Perhaps he did not want to subject the crash of the Nationalist Party in the 1960s to the mockery of his teenage sons. I don't know. All I have is a picture and the speculation it has triggered.

There is another picture of a dark-haired woman. And one of a little trap, the type drawn by a donkey or a horse.

People didn't carry cameras in their pockets in the 1930s and '40s. Even when I first took an interest in taking pictures in the 1960s, photography was expensive. The film had to be left with a chemist to be developed. You paid for every print, even for pictures of half your shoe, taken accidentally.

Photographs were called snaps, a term coined by the sellers of cheap cameras to suggest that taking pictures was easy, but the act of taking a picture in Barney's day would have been almost ceremonial. Photographs were for special occasions, like First Communion. They were taken in studios with props and backdrops, and subjects were encouraged to look grim and thoughtful.

There had been several attempts to popularise photography through the Box Brownie and the Instamatic. There was an old camera in our house with a concertina, retractable lens, so somebody must have been taking the art more seriously decades before me – but who? It was a Kodak Vest Pocket, perhaps dating back to about 1920.

Maybe this was the camera that took those few little pictures Barney had kept in a drawer, but I doubt it. I never saw either of my parents take a picture or even hold a camera. The Vest Pocket had floated, perhaps as a gift or legacy, into a family which had no use for it.

The few snaps it took now live on as portraits in *in memoriam* cards, a purpose the original photographer had probably not even considered.

Media

'Sure, what are you talking about? Isn't it there in black and white?' Barney had, for a long time, believed what he read in the newspaper. Until he started to read more than one paper, he did not notice that they often disagreed and therefore, that the matter being detailed in print hardly fixes it in history. Every morning in life he took *The Irish News*. On Sundays, he read *The Sunday Press* until it died. And in these, he saw the world much as he understood it, reflected back to him.

But he could not for long escape the diversification of media through the arrival of local radio and the London tabloids. Then it was not one of his arrogant sons but a newspaper headline, or the voice of a newsreader, which challenged his understanding. He was affronted by their scurrilous lies.

So the media became a channel for his anger in more complex ways than it had before.

In the past, he would have read the safe, affirming papers, and the anger that flared in him at the outrages by political figures would have been in line with the paper's editorial approach. The paper would be on his side. He would sit in his armchair by the fire, his reading glasses low on his nose so that he could see over them, the paper at arm's length so that he could make out the print more clearly, and he would growl pleasurably, with the relaxed ease of a man who knows that a great newspaper concurs with his every opinion.

His reactions were more complicated when the story that riled him was delivered by a voice that was detached, patriarchal or even enthusiastic.

'Would you listen to that eejit there,' he would say, snapping at the radio as if the personal affront of a presenter's naivety could be promptly hurled back at him through the air.

He had previously been able to think of the media as friendly and coherent. He had been able to select the papers and stations which endorsed his own rural, Catholic, Gaelic roots, and to feel at home with the opinions and perspectives he found there.

But the media fragmented and he no longer felt that it was there to reassure him. It seemed, on the contrary, to specialise in annoying him. So he would crouch in front of the television, ready to pounce on its lies, and all the more eagerly when rioting and killing in the streets around him were the substance of the evening news, and he could be confident of knowing the details better than some English journalist, since he had talked to a man in a bar who had seen the whole thing.

Television was a marvel. We were late getting one and right up to the 1960s I would have gone to a neighbour's house on a Saturday evening to watch *The Lone Ranger*.

The first intimation for me that the boundary between television and the real world could be crossed was when the Lone Ranger visited Belfast. A friend of Barney's, an RUC man, had himself photographed in uniform, standing beside the masked man.

This was as confusing for me as if the Lone Ranger had leapt out of the set and proven to be only six inches tall. Shouldn't the policeman have demanded that he take his mask off?

That picture sat on a shelf in the corner of our living room for many years, and was perhaps only removed when the Troubles started in the late '60s when it would have made good sense in Catholic working class areas not to have a photograph of a policeman on display in your home.

Barney himself should have understood that radio and television are just human voices, voices that can be as undependable as those you hear on the street. Isn't that what the photograph of the Lone Ranger and the RUC man proved? It should not have been a new surprise to him every day in life, that reporters and presenters dissented from his earnest convictions; but then again, every contradiction he faced in life shocked him as much as if it was the first. He never got used to others seeing the world differently.

My earliest memory of radio is of the broadcasts from Hungary that he listened to in 1956 during the Russian invasion. What was this but the raw anguish of beleaguered people, in all its passion and frailty, as opposed to the authoritative poise of Soviet propaganda?

He must have heard plenty of propaganda during the war too, so how had he acquired this assumption that there was a dependable source anywhere? In the end he trusted only what was local. The home place, as he understood it, was where neighbours agreed with each other. He felt he belonged among people who valued what was Irish before what was British, what was Nationalist before what was Unionist, and what they heard on the street or in the bar before what they were told by the television or a newspaper.

There had been a time when Barney could avoid all challenges in the media, but as he grew older and the media changed, and his conservative simplicities were expiring, it was harder to be safe from contradiction, even when he was alone in his living room. Yet he always had the television on. I'd visit and he would expect me to sit and watch alongside him, to be the one who could share his contempt for the stupidity of what was being said, even in advertisements.

'What sort of fools do they take us for? Sure who in their right mind would pay a tenner for junk like that? I don't know what the world is coming to.'

Hats

The number of times I had been sent to school in the rain, wrapped up in ghastly clobber! My mother had an old scarf that was like a tube with sealed ends. You could punch in one of the ends and roll it over a wee boy's head and cover his ears, then wrap the rest around his neck. It didn't matter what it looked like, so long as he was warm and dry.

For Barney, the hat was only functional. If you look at old photographs of life in rural or urban Ireland fifty years ago, you see that everyone in them wears one. There is some limited variation among the hats. Bowlers and even stetsons are common but most common of all is the plain flat duncher. These hats had a job, and it was not to advertise the charms of the wearer, though they may have spoken about his social standing. The hat was expected to keep the head warm. The duncher perhaps survived longer than other hats because it is less of a nuisance when taken off.

The duncher was the hat for a modest and practical man who knew his place, who didn't want to be thought ridiculous or flash. It was a cap that could be rolled up and put in the pocket of your coat and therefore not be separated from it when you hung it up, and less likely to be lost.

A duncher for Barney was also a handy mop. He would wipe the mist from the inside of his windscreen with it in the morning. That was part of the ritual of preparing for the moment when the ignition would be tried.

He only ever wore a plain duncher or a little Tweed stingy brim, a bit like a trilby.

Headwear is always dangerously suggestive of ostentation – a sin in Barney's world. So a hat, paradoxically, had to be as fastidiously chosen to avoid the suggestion of glamour as any ball gown ever was to attain it.

In old age, Barney saw only practicality in the hat and would not have understood a man declining to wear one but for a good practical reason. Indeed, he often wore a duncher indoors. Why not? Who was to be offended? For all I know he wore it in bed.

Shoes

Barney was keen that I should look respectable, at least on a Sunday. The fact that I rarely do, probably stems from a reaction to his ardent efforts.

I can recall the feel of his wet comb across my scalp at the kitchen sink as he readied me for Mass. He had a problem with the fact that my hair fell forward and he was determined to have this one out with nature. Mine should go straight back over the top of my head, like his. And he eulogised about the value of well polished shoes. 'You could go for a job interview in a T-shirt, but if the boss sees that you have clean and well polished shoes, he will know that you're dependable.'

No he won't. He will know that I have bought new shoes for the interview.

My father belonged to a generation of men who did not distinguish themselves by dress. The only categories he knew were scruffy and tidy. The limit of variation in tidiness was a choice between brown shoes and black.

The basic outfit was a suit, jacket and trousers, and he would have sneered at the fashionable embellishments of these. Jackets got longer. Much as they widened and narrowed, he always understood that there was a right size for a lapel, and time has confirmed this.

Back in 1920, when Barney was six years old, some children went barefoot to school. Barney was not one of them or he would surely have been moaning about it still in his eighties. His entire attitude to the world of his own children was a scowl, and if there had been another contrast to be made between their comfort and his lack of it, he would have made it.

Then again, perhaps this conviction that shoes were the best indicator of a man's worth grew out of his early days, when leather would have been the mark of wealth.

Barney was almost fanatical about the need to polish shoes. We would all be sent to the kitchen on a Saturday night to get the polish and brushes out from under the sink and he would instruct us on the correct technique.

There were other marks of respectability that he valued; the tie, the wristwatch and the cut of the hair. He thought of them all as substitutes for a good suit.

That thinking sounds to me like a relic of the day when a young man might be compared to another with nice clothes but bare feet, when being properly dressed was never an option in reach of the poor, and a parent dressing a son for the world always had to choose one shortcut or another. Perhaps Barney's father had been smart enough to know where to make the best investment in a child's job prospects. Perhaps Barney himself thought he was still judged by how well his own children were shod.

Barney mostly wore only two kinds of shoe, the brogue and the derby, and only in two colours, black and brown. Later he discovered Hush Puppies, but there was a question to be resolved about whether they were fit wear for work. The suede could provide no evidence of a man's strong elbow and clean spit. It didn't speak well of character.

The brogue was a worker's shoe. It came out of the bog. Its pattern of punched holes is said to have provided drainage for a man who walked over swampy peat. This I doubt. More likely they aired the sweaty foot of a man who couldn't afford a fresh pair of socks every day.

But, in Barney's youth the brogue was not a shoe to be worn in town. It was a heavy durable shoe with a nailed leather sole.

Shoes, which for my father embodied respectability, have become for me a symbol of restraint and formality, and I sense that the roots of this are in Donegal in the 1920s, when Barney first learned to wear them and to see them as distinguishing him from poorer children around him who didn't. Since I have reacted against his obsession with shoes, I have always been scruffily shod. I am the making of my father, if not to his design.

Eating Out

For Barney, going to someone else's house for your dinner would have made as much sense as going there for a bath. Some things were just done at home. I doubt he ever dined out more than half a dozen times in all his life, not even in a restaurant. Eating wasn't pleasure – well not a pleasure to be shared. It was private. He understood the cafe as a place you could go for a quick meal at the heart of a working day. It was a public convenience.

The modern notion of visiting a restaurant in the spirit in which you would enter a church or an art gallery, would have been, to him, pretentious and wasteful.

He would have judged a meal by how close it was to what he got at home. Paying money for food that you expected would be different from what you got at home would have been like buying a coat because it fitted someone else.

Life had taught Barney what a proper fried egg was like. It was crisp around the fringe, everybody knew that. It was caramelised below – or, in his terms, burnt. The yolk was soft but not runny, and the white flesh of the egg had firmed up into a rim around that yolk. If there was adventure in his cooking, it was in the daring flip of a fried egg that slapped the yolk onto the hot pan, where it defied the expectation that it would splat and spread, but, when you flipped it back, had merely acquired a milky film.

It would only have annoyed him to find in a cafe that eggs were served in consistencies beyond the range he trusted. He would have learnt what an egg was from his mother and he would probably not have had to teach his wife – my mother – how he'd like his done.

Everybody did things the same way, if they did them right. For instance, who ever heard of you having to wash a frying pan after one use? In our house, and in most houses, the frying pan sat on the range or on the ring, with a reassuringly even and congealed, perhaps slightly speckled, smearing of lard on it. That meant that today's eggs tasted of yesterday's bacon or black pudding, and that was good.

He had an idiosyncratic way of buttering a slice of bread. He would hold it flat on his left hand and draw the knife across with his right. Maybe this was the method of a boy who had taken his meal outdoors, in the field, haymaking, and a reminder that, in his natural state, he did not belong in a house.

Eating was functional.

If my mother had to sleep through Saturday, I often got the job of heating Barney's soup for him when he came in at lunchtime. He frequently arrived back in a snarly mood, or at least a sullen one. And even if he was, by his own standards, cheerful, he was still impatient and brusque. My job was to open a can of soup, add water if it was Campbell's and not if it was Heinz, heat it until it was not quite boiling and serve it to him at the kitchen table with buttered bread and a cup of tea. This was a purely functional service, like helping him off with his boots might have been. He hadn't it in him not to be intimidating, or I hadn't it in me not to be intimidated by him. I suspect my wariness of him simply made him worse and frustrated his efforts to be convivial, as much as his tetchiness frustrated my efforts to relax in his company and enjoy him.

I always felt I was in the way.

And the food I served him looked joyless and drab and he ate it as if he was simply fuelling himself.

Most days the children ate as they came home from school or work, but on Sundays the whole family ate together. I loved my mother's stews and soups. I loved how she took yesterday's leftover mashed potato and fried it brown. I loved the new potatoes cooked in their jackets and served in one huge bowl in the middle of the table. I loved peeling the potatoes and licking off the remnants that stuck to the thumb. I watched Barney peeling his to learn how to wield a knife; he always cut towards himself and with the deftness of someone who was remembering more dangerous work with sharper tools. I even loved eating the skins afterwards, despite having taken such trouble to remove them. You had to, because the sheen on the surface of a well peeled new potato has a texture like wax and, as proof of God's good will, is designed to receive salt and butter directly. I have never found food of any kind that pleases me more.

The table, however, was a place of added discipline, of constant reminders to use your fork properly and not to be talking, but none of this for me overturned the enjoyment of food, when it was good; that is, when it was fresh and simple.

I can almost forgive Barney's contempt for his tinned soup on days when no one had time to make a proper broth with barley and a bone.

Sex

As children we called them the soppy bits, the scenes in which the cowboy kissed the saloon tart and the action stalled. We shared with Barney our exasperation with sex. He went 'tsk' and, if the grapple developed, would say, 'turn that rubbish off,' or later, 'turn over to the other side and see if there is anything decent on there.'

I don't know if he enjoyed sex on television when his children were not watching with him. If Barney had any strong interest in erotica, he concealed it well.

His regular magazine was *John Bull*, which carried pictures of healthy young women stretching themselves in tight jumpers. It was while scrutinising one of those pictures that I discovered my first twinge of lust, though I didn't understand why the curves of the woman's chest were so fascinating.

But Barney wanted to avoid sex mainly to spare him embarrassment in front of his children and not, I suppose now, out of any squeamishness. I discovered recently in conversation with a woman in her eighties that she had assumed that oral sex was an interaction that could be accomplished over the phone. The correction appalled her. She had never had a notion to do that herself.

I never had a conversation with Barney that would clear up the question of whether he really knew what other people do. One day I found him sitting on his hospital bed watching *Baywatch*. I took this programme for soft porn, since most of the characters were in swimsuits. Barney hardly looked away when I came into the room, so we sat together quietly following the large-breasted women prancing back and forth across the beach. Finally he said to me, 'It's a good programme this.'

He appeared to have only just discovered the series, and not to be aware of how it featured in popular humour. I don't think he had noticed that it was styled to titillate. Was that an effect of ageing? Or maybe heaving bosoms and sturdy thighs were familiar to him from the cinema of the 1940s.

I never thought of my father as having a sexual nature, nor wanted to. When I reached puberty – late – he was turning fifty, so he was younger than I am now. I do not expect a man in his fifties to have outgrown his desire for physical intimacy.

Indeed, in full old age, in his mid-eighties, Barney spoke of one of the young female doctors who tended him in hospital, being attracted to him.

In the same way that he had never lost confidence that he could fight – though he never did – he also continued to imagine that he could appeal to young women.

My mother did have a sexual element to her humour and demeanour even late in life, and oddly it is less discomfiting for me to contemplate her sexual nature than his.

Once, on holiday in the cottage in Port Salon, she fell asleep drunk and complained the next day that Barney had put her to bed without unfastening her bra.

She joked, 'A gentleman always unfastens a lady's bra when she passes out on him.' Perhaps she was quoting a joke she had heard in London during the war.

Barney was not asexual but he would never have consciously allowed his sons to see anything of his sexual interests, and he did not want to know anything about theirs either.

He was civil and formal with our girlfriends.

When, in my thirties, I phoned him to ask if I could come and stay the night with a girl I had met in Donegal a few days earlier, he told me to fuck off. I could do what I liked but not under his roof.

Patricia, the wife of his brother Michael, told me a story from the days just after the war, when the three brothers, Barney, Michael and George were drinking with the women they would marry. At one point, Michael spilt a drink that splashed Patricia. George leapt to his feet brandishing his fists and insisted that he would not tolerate any woman being so insulted in his company.

George, and perhaps the others, believed in a chivalry which entitled a man to punch any other man who offended any woman, even his own girlfriend, even by accident.

Maybe Barney had inherited from that touchy family background a sense that impropriety towards a woman was risky.

But Barney was appalling sometimes – and not himself. I cringe to recall the one occasion I saw him make an ass of himself expressing a sexual interest in a woman. She was forty years younger than him. Yet it was an expression of plain voyeurism rather than raunchy greed. It was a remark that seems coy in a way.

This was at a Christmas party when, in one of those moments in which the volume of chatter unaccountably drops, he was heard to ask a question that might occur to a man who is imagining comforts he knows he will never enjoy again.

He said, 'Do you wear your knickers in bed?'

When Barney was in his early eighties, and passing most of his time alone, a social worker looking in on him after a spell in hospital, suggested he go to the day centre.

'Sure what's there but a load of ould dolls?' he said.

This delusion about his age had two effects. It cut him off from women and it left him entirely unprepared for death, an event of whose relative imminence he seems to have lived in ignorance.

He died at eighty-seven, as argumentative at the end as he had ever been, but withdrawn, in the sense that he had no further use for his intelligence, indeed no use for his life, a loss that perhaps explains his colossal appetite for alcohol.

Part of the problem of old age is that people give up any expectation of being surprised.

If the man next door has buried his wife under the patio, well, you know by a certain age that that is the sort of thing some men do.

Men Hugging

I often wonder about Barney's 1950s digs when I see the painting of medical students by the Belfast artist Gerard Dillon, with three of them sharing a bed under a patchwork quilt. That is how the boys in our family slept until they were into their teens.

Barney was never affectionate with men. Men of his age never were.

He saw footballers leaping on each other as an incomprehensible marvel.

'Would you ever look at that?'

'It doesn't mean that they are gay,' you might explain.

'Did I say it did?'

In fact, much of his sentimentality was directed at men. He would go almost weepy at the sound of Eddie Calvert playing 'Oh! My Pa-pa'.

'That's the man with the golden trumpet,' he said, aglow with admiration.

'Is it really made of gold? Solid gold?'

'Ach!'

A song he taught us as children was Patsy Fagan: 'Hello, Patsy Fagan, You're the apple of my eye.'

And I often heard him comment of some man on television that he was handsome or good looking. He would never have thought of these observations as belonging on a spectrum of sexual interest.

And when he wished to express warmth for another man, he would do it obliquely. He would display an exaggerated gruffness, expecting you to know that this was not real gruffness, but that it was – between yourselves – encoded with love.

On the night I returned from seven years away from home, mostly in England and in India, I went up to his bedroom to say hello. He sat up in his pyjamas with a grin on his face and said, 'I am a better fucking man than you are, any day of the week.'

His affection always came disguised as aggression. Barney liked to assert that he had power over you. Intimacy and affection had to be laced with a threat – a deniable threat, of course – and shielded against emotion. But if he was stronger than you and still loved you, wasn't that an even greater compliment?

In dealing with sons and other children, he would only show interest which secured that power. I suspect that when he was with other men, above him in the pecking order, he understood that he was to cheerfully position himself more abjectly, playful and amusing.

None of this, as he understood things, was specific to himself. He saw around him a world in which men took their places in hierarchies.

Foreigners

My father grew up in a white Ireland in which all speech he heard, other than on the wireless, was in the local accent of Donegal and Derry city. A good plain earthy accent it is too, with a touch of musicality but without extravagance. Barney would have been twenty-seven years old when voices he had known from the cinema came here and surrounded him. The Yanks in Derry gave him a job. I know nothing of what he actually did for them. I just know that this was a time in his life when his hopes for himself grew, hopes that were later dashed by that incredible run of children, six in eight years.

I wonder if he acquired an American accent for a time back then, the way I did myself as a little boy watching cowboy films. I'd say he shook it off quickly when the soldiers went home after the war.

He did twang his inflections at times. This might have been the adoption of a drawl.

If there was a period which would have acquainted Barney's generation with sudden cultural change and an ethnic spread it was the early 1940s. He would have been friendly with boys with Texan yawps, New York Jews and African Americans. I'm guessing that is why I never heard him use racist words of the kind that came easily to other men his age.

Black journalists and soldiers in Belfast were called Sambo and Nigger, at least when their backs were turned. Barney never left Ireland in his life, was never on a plane, but never had that spontaneous bemusement at the foreigner.

Yet he was naive. When my brother worked for a time in Belgium, Barney explained to me that 'It's different out foreign.' You had to take particular care of your tools. The whole world beyond the shore was 'out foreign', a uniformly dangerous place.

Human Rights

There was a good Barney and a drunk Barney, and the good Barney would not have harmed anyone – I don't think. As a bar manager he must often have had to make decisions which annoyed people, but I doubt that he was unjust.

He certainly hadn't accumulated the wealth that falls more easily to those who cheat. He was not a criminal. But his sense of how to deal with people was drawn from a woollier sense of justice than the term 'human rights' implied. I think he doubted that he had any rights himself. He did not think he was in a position to accord to others the right to anything but common civility. Why would you do harm to someone who has done no harm to you? He would have summed it up like that.

He liked people and he was jovial. That was the height of it. He was not, in this, adhering to any principle or demanding of others that they should.

One of the words of which he was most contemptuous, was 'entitle'. He would say, 'Listen, that's not the way the world works.'

The world was unfair and could not be changed. That was a basic fact that you had to learn to live with. It was simply ridiculous to think you could change that and force the world to conform to your notions of justice. To argue otherwise was to betray the kind of stupidity that would one day get you into deep trouble, that would invite others to abuse you.

This fact of life was the thing that angered him most.

Though he was determined to be in the right in every argument, he told me that being in the right counted for nothing in an unjust world. He didn't believe in rights in the way he didn't believe in fairies.

And if you were dealing with the law you were obviously going to be walked over by people stronger than you, unless you were very lucky. Things working out in your favour could only be a fluke. And that being the case, every advantage you could play would be legitimate.

If young lads threatened his peace, he would have seen it as the job of the police to 'take hold of the buggers and give them a good kick up the arse.' But he would never, I think, have called the police, unless directly affected, for that would have gone against the old code that you don't welch on others. And if the police entered his life with any query, he would regard that simply as an intrusion. Once, before the Troubles, two policemen on patrol stopped to look at a fire I had built in our garden.

'What did they want?' said Barney. 'What business is it of theirs?'

Being in the right counted for nothing if you had got a knock on the head or been cheated at cards. 'Sure you should have known better.' It was not knowledge of your rights that steered you safely through this world, it was ordinary savvy, a grasp of where danger lies.

Religion

I don't think Barney would have made much of atheists – not emphatic atheists anyway. He grew up in a conservative religious culture in which a state of doubt was allowed for as the norm. The church's advice to those who queried the existence of God was to pray for help. But I wonder if many followed that injunction too seriously. Men of his generation were only devout in church. And as a boy, when I watched him pray, I found him impenetrable. I could not have told from the expression on his face, as he kneeled in the pew after communion, whether he was talking to God about his doubts or counting up his debts. He might have been a wholly abstracted mystic, or he might have been asleep.

Both my mother and he were acquainted with the *Rubaiyat of Omar Khayyam* but that tells me nothing. Much of it reads like a scowl against belief and a light reader might fail to observe that there is anything more to it. 'The moving finger writes, and having writ moves on ...' My mother would say that at the kitchen sink. Pure fatalism? Maybe it was her way of expressing her disappointment with life, reassuring herself that she had never had it in her power to shape it differently.

I don't know what lines my father favoured. 'And much as wine has played the infidel ...'

There is a lot about wine in the *Rubaiyat* and by the end of his life my father had put more faith in the consolations of drink than of anything else. Yet, up to middle age, he went on his knees in church, though a little half-heartedly, sometimes with one knee half raised or his bum still grazing the seat so that he could restore himself to a sitting position without anyone really noticing him move.

He wanted his children to believe and he was exasperated by the decline in their interest in church in their teenage years. What did he believe? I doubt if he ever asked himself that question. He believed what he wanted to believe, for as long as he wanted to believe it.

Once he explained to me how Donegal came to be covered in peat. It was the sludge that had settled after the Flood, when God had washed all life from the Earth, save whatever had got onto the Ark.

Yet, when we were children he challenged our own simple faith, and enjoyed doing that. Did Cain marry a monkey or his sister? If there is life on other planets, did Jesus go there too? Will he come back for the monkeys when they have evolved further?

He knew his prayer book and catechism but not much of the Bible, and the question of whether any of it was literally true did not cost him a moment's sleep, at least not in my memory.

Religion was a body of information that had been given to him, of which he made some minimal use, as the need arose, but which taxed his concern no more than did astrophysics or the financial markets.

My mother, by her own account, did take theology seriously enough to reject it when it asked her to believe things which she thought were daft. She worked as a night sister in a hospital and went straight to bed when she got home on a Sunday morning, so it was Barney's job to take us to Mass. 'I've already been, at the hospital,' she would say. It was only when she was close to death, thirty years later, and had confessed her sins to a young priest, that she shared the secret with me that she had given up religion in the 1950s. She explained that the breaking point for her had been a doctrine of the Assumption of the Virgin Mary.

She would have made that decision in about 1954, when we were living in Ballycastle to be near her mother, and while Barney was working in Belfast and would not have been around often on a Sunday morning, Belfast bars having been busiest on a Saturday night.

Who knows what complex of loyalties she was challenging? Was she telling Barney that she was going to Mass when she wasn't?

And is there another clue in the strange fact that I was baptised twice, once at home on the day I was born, presumably because I was a premature twin and therefore in some danger, and then again, formally, but not for a year-and-a-half.

If my parents had been keen to be seen by their neighbours as conscientious Catholics, surely they would have moved faster? When she did take us to the font, my mother was again pregnant, nearly seven months pregnant. This means that we were baptised as close to the latest possible date if she wasn't to be bringing three children to the font, the twins upstaged by the next boy.

There might have been some bland practical reason for the procrastination. We were safe from the tedium of Limbo after that early private ritual, presumably in her bedroom, but still, it seems to signal a lack of enthusiasm for the faith.

The young priest that brought my mother back into the church in her last days had been happy to absolve her of her sins without insisting that she reverse her opinions on the Assumption.

I can't imagine that Barney concerned himself much with the incompatibility of spirit and matter or that he would have quarrelled with church doctrine. Whether or not he believed that the Virgin Mary had been assumed physically into Heaven, would not change the course of a day's work, lighten or add to his troubles. He had enough to worry about, and he would have been completely bewildered by anyone whose thinking on the matter, one way or the other, had any bearing on how they lived their lives.

Yet maybe I have misread him; indeed, how could I have read him right when he said so little?

I think that he simply lost interest in religion. Or perhaps he just had too many embarrassing sins to confess to be able to make his way lightly back into the fold. Such a drinker must have accumulated a few. But after his children had grown up he stopped going to Mass himself. For a time he went alone without us, and then gave up altogether: which suggests that his main reason for going was to help pass religion on to us. If there was something more to his motivation, it was not enough.

He did have a meditative streak. I have no idea how he acquired a love of silence, unless it is genetic, but he had a gift for being able to sit contentedly for hours alone in his garden.

He was no natural mystic or contemplative. He had almost no emotional control that I saw, at least in his dealings with other people, and yet his core was often still.

And he sat alone often in his old age, partly because his company was so difficult for others to endure. He would complain about being left alone but he would make his own company so awkward that I would leave as soon as I decently could. I suspect my company was as difficult for him as his was for me. It would be some consolation to think so.

He nurtured some religious sentiment again after my mother died, when he said that he prayed to her. I asked him then why he didn't go to Mass and he said he had never liked it since they had done away with the Latin – in 1964.

Barney had achieved an indifference to the church. He would mock the over-religious, the people who 'chewed the altar rails'. He sneered at the goodie types who used religion, he assumed, to let you know they were better than you.

But he was too deeply rooted in a peasant religious culture to shake it off. He knew what to do at a wake. He could mutter his rosary responses without cynicism.

He did not like the smart aleck who disdained that. He would have thought it self-indulgent and cruel to try to undermine the faith of those who took comfort in prayer and the minimal observance of their religious duties.

And he might have been a happier man in his closing years if he had taken some comfort there himself. For whatever reason, he didn't. It wasn't a refusal to believe that God would hear his prayers. I think he just felt so far removed from God that it would be presumptuous to bother Him. He was proud like that.

So when he was on his deathbed, we did not know whether to send for a priest for him, whether he would welcome him or turn away from him. Then a nurse told us that the chaplain had been to see him and that everything was 'done'.

That settled it for us.

Months later I met Ken Newell, a Presbyterian minister that I knew through my work. He said, 'How is Barney?'

I was bewildered but told him that Barney was dead. How did he know him?

Ken said that I had mentioned to him one day when I was distracted, that my father was in hospital. When visiting another patient, he had sought him out and Barney had been pleased to pray with him.

'I offered him the Aaronic blessing,' said Ken.

I heard that as the 'ironic blessing' and thought it appropriate.

I rarely, in adult life, felt that Barney had an expertise that I would need to draw on other than his being himself, his knowledge of himself.

Many times I would like to have asked him; what does it feel like to know that death is near? Are their consolations in ageing?

From the manner in which he faced death, agitated and refusing it, I surmise that he never engaged with the apprehension of it at all, that he somehow imagined he would never face it, that he felt it an outrageous injustice that it was before him.

Once, when he was in hospital, I urged him to look after himself better and to stop drinking. I said, 'you could have another twenty years; people do now.' And he did look amazed at the thought, so he must have reconciled himself to having much less time than that.

And I wondered – and wonder still – how someone who knows that death is near can occasionally smile and be interested in things.

Maybe his only hope of facing death with grace or resignation lay in his losing his interest in this world. He didn't care about very much when he was in his eighties.

Only small things angered him then, though they angered him greatly.

But he could not let go when he was near the end. He fretted and clung to people. I would go into the hospital ward and he would frantically call the nurse to say I was here now and could take him home. He was like a child evading school by pretending to be sick, though a man evading death by pretending to be well.

He reached his lips to the cheek of a nurse to kiss her hungrily, and I was reminded of a television image of Yasser Arafat doing the same thing, as he was being lifted into the flight that would take him to his death in Paris.

Barney could have gone more easily. He had only to let go. His breathing was laboured. The hospital would not tranquillise for fear of killing him outright. He exhausted himself pushing for breath. I hope that if I am ever like that I will be wise enough to slip away. He has taught me by example how not to live and how not to die.

I am trying to remember a funeral that Barney and I would have attended together. His Derry/Donegal culture was detailed on dealing with death, enjoyed waking and burying the dead.

We went to his brother Michael's funeral Mass together but not to the wake. We did not inspect Michael in his coffin and we did not join in the usual gathering and chatter. The wake does something important and does it well. It turns the seriousness of honouring the dead into light socialising. A wake is never a miserable occasion. It is always full of laughter.

Barney would have known that, but if he joined in, I never saw it. And so I learnt waking skills from others, skills that it is more common for a man to learn from his father.

He was shy, I think, though I never, when he was alive, thought so. Perhaps he only functioned well among people with a drink in him. And, for all that the lore about wakes always describes the punch and the pipes, a priest friend tells me they are rarely drunken occasions.

The wake was devised for people like Barney. It was a social mechanism for deflating excessive reverence, for taking the ceremonies for the dead away from the church. Maybe Barney was at many wakes without me. But when he crossed thresholds, like those at wakes, he probably expected to be more relaxed, more loud and even more irreverent than custom dictated, so he was wiser staying away.

He lay in his own coffin with rosary beads entwined in his fingers. No one stepped forward to say how ridiculous that was. Decisions like that seem to take themselves. Tradition is like nature – it just does its own thing. Someone, probably the undertaker, would later have had the job of unclasping those hands to get the beads back for their owner.

He didn't look like himself. His cheeks had been patted back into shape by someone who hadn't known him, flattened against the bone, whereas they should have been a little saggy. I gave him a blue jacket which made him look like a barman or a club doorman from an earlier age, which perhaps was right in a way, though I doubt he would ever have worn that colour by choice.

Hundreds came, including boys I had been to school with and hadn't seen since, now middle-aged. There was no heat in the house because you keep the air cool round a corpse.

I walked the length of the street I had played in as a child and had shuffled along to school on wet days, propping a corner of his coffin and measuring my steps. It was easier work than pushing his car, or holding still on the handlebars of his bike while he ground down on the pedals, cursing my weight. It was the first time he had ever been at my shoulder without telling me that, whatever it was I was doing, I was doing it wrong.